Medical Journalism

Medical Journalism

EXPOSING FACT, FICTION, FRAUD

Dr. Ragnar Levi

IOWA STATE UNIVERSITY PRESS / AMES

Ragnar Levi, M.D., award-winning Medical Editor, has a background in both medicine and journalism. Since 1992, Dr. Levi has been the Executive Editor of Science & Practice, a newsletter recognized with an award by the American Medical Writers Association in 1996. As a journalist, he has published numerous critical articles on health care and the pitfalls of medical communication. Dr. Levi is also the author of a monograph, in Swedish, on evidence-based health care. Queries and suggestions regarding this book may be sent to the author at: levi@pi.se

© 2001 Ragnar Levi
All rights reserved

Cartoons: © Gunnar Kaj and Ragnar Levi

All characters and events portrayed in the cartoons are fictional and any resemblance to real people or incidents is purely coincidental.

Iowa State University Press
2121 South State Avenue, Ames, Iowa 50014

Orders: 1-800-862-6657
Office: 1-515-292-0140
Fax: 1-515-292-3348
Website: www.isupress.com

Authorization to photocopy items for internal or personal use, or the internal or personal use of specific clients, is granted by Iowa State University Press, provided that the base fee of $.10 per copy is paid directly to the Copyright Clearance Center, 222 Rosewood Drive, Danvers, MA 01923. For those organizations that have been granted a photocopy license by CCC, a separate system of payments has been arranged. The fee code for users of the Transactional Reporting Service is 0-8138-0303-9/01 $.10.

∞ Printed on acid-free paper in the United States of America

First edition, 2001

Library of Congress Cataloging-in-Publication Data

Levi, Ragnar.
    Medical journalism : exposing fact, fiction, fraud / Ragnar Levi.—
1st ed.
        p. ; cm.
Originally published: Lund : Studentlitteratur, c2000.
Includes bibliographical references and index.
    ISBN 0-8138-0303-9 (alk. paper)
1. Journalism, Medical. I. Title.
PN4784.M4 L48 2001
070.4'4961—dc21

The last digit is the print number: 9 8 7 6 5 4 3 2 1

Contents

To the memory of Piu Helena Olsson (1958–2000)

Foreword

Deborah Blum, Pulitzer Prize–winning science writer
and professor of journalism at University of Wisconsin–Madison

Early in my life as a science journalist, I wrote a story about the side effects of chemotherapy. Some were startling to me—such as the risk of secondary cancers—and I thought that readers might be as uninformed as I had been. As it turned out, I was terrifyingly correct on that point. The day after the story ran, a woman called me to say that her doctor had never told her about the downside of her treatment and that she had dropped out of treatment and was trusting her fate to me. "But I'm a journalist," I said desperately, at one point in the conversation. "I'm not a doctor."

The problem was that, at that moment, she trusted me more. And there I was, assuming that everyone knew not to trust a journalist. After several days, I managed to line her up with another, more forthright oncologist, and she resumed treatment. That was about ten years ago. But I've kept that edgy, uncomfortable awareness: of the power that medicine and medical research has over people's lives, of how ill-informed many of us are, and of how dismayingly often the media can be the only source of real information.

The uneasy state of medical knowledge—which Ragnar Levi addresses so compellingly in this book—extends far beyond the individual doctor-patient relationship. Medical researchers remain poor, often reluctant communicators with the public. Medical journalists therefore assume an ever more important role in not only sharing information but also announcing its worth. So journalistic accuracy is crucial and the need for integrity in reporting is absolute.

Books like this one are therefore not just interesting but imperative. If the media are to be the public's primary source of information on medical progress, new technology, and the ways that research may extend or shorten life, we must understand not only the message but the messenger. Science and medicine may well be the most powerful forces shaping—and altering—our lives today, so the need to understand that power is self-evident. But we have been slower to recognize the need to understand the role of those who communicate science and medicine. And yet, as eloquently illustrated here, evaluating the storyteller's credibility may be as important to our health as evaluating the story. How seriously should we take the announcement of a new "miracle" drug, the doomsday tale of a newly emerged virus, the risks and benefits of biotechnology?

The late American astronomer—and lover of scientific communication—Carl Sagan once challenged science journalists to find the balance between wonder and skepticism. Implicit in that charge was his worry that we have tended to be heavy on the gee-whiz wonder and light on the skepticism about research. To strike the right balance, as Levi points out, we must examine all practitioners with an eye to identifying "fact, fiction, and fraud." In other words, let us be realistic about the need for skepticism about medicine *and* about medical journalism—and let us employ that skepticism not merely to criticize but to improve.

I have great respect for many—even most—in the community of science and medical journalism. I've spent years in that community, as a newspaper science reporter, a magazine writer, and a writer of popular-science books. And I know that against a background of often-reluctant sources, strong pressure from the medical/pharmaceutical industry, and the rapid turnover demands of journalism, most reporters do a remarkable job. For the most part, the public gets a balanced viewpoint; they have become more savvy thanks to good reporting, and perhaps more cynical too, but certainly better able to evaluate medical advances—or the lack of them.

A book like this one, which gathers together first-class research and the perspectives of some of the best science/medical journalists in the world, will certainly help raise journalistic standards. That alone is a worthwhile accomplishment. But beyond such merit, this is a remarkably clear-sighted exploration of the power and perils of medical journalism. There is much to be learned here, for working journalists, for student journalists, and for all of us, in the end, ordinary people struggling not to be blown astray by the prevailing winds of medical progress.

Preface

"Cancer Treatment Promises Hope." "Common Drug Kills Thousands." "New Drug Raises Hope for Alzheimer's Victims." "Research Will Eradicate Diabetes." Headlines like these grab readers' attention every day. But how accurate and truthful are the stories behind the headlines? How important are they? And where did they originate—from "spin" doctors or medical doctors?

Since most journalists subscribe to professional ideals, readers expect the stories to be true and significant. This distinguishes journalism from, say, the worlds of advertising, fiction, and show business. However, at times it is difficult to tell these worlds apart.

The public is getting used to seeing entertainment and advertising masquerade as journalism. The proliferation of infomercials—ads that purport to be informative—is a case in point. Journalists and scriptwriters alike know that good stories, whether factual or fictional, revolve around a few basic human themes. When it comes to the crunch, fascinating medical stories—like most soap operas—are all about death, fear, hope, power, sex, love, and compassion.

However, the best medical reporters offer their readers much more than just thrills. While telling good stories, they also manage to weigh the information they receive, separate fact from fiction, and serve their audience with probing, critical journalism. They prove that you can be provocative, titillating, entertaining, and still get the facts right.

This book is for those who care about improving medical journalism—for the reporters, editors, readers, listeners, viewers, scientists, and health professionals who believe it is possible to carry medical reporting forward, despite the constraints of tight deadlines, editorial ignorance, and pressed budgets.

Avoiding all the pitfalls of medical reporting outlined in this book is admittedly utopian. Not even the most experienced medical journalist will spot every half-truth, inflated hope, or false alarm. The pressures inherent in running most media corporations do not always allow reporters to be as critical as they might aspire to be. However, asking critical questions and avoiding some of the worst hazards is a good beginning.

How to tell fact from fiction on the medical beat is the fundamental journalistic challenge explored in this book. Distinguishing between fact and fable need not be as complicated and time-consuming as one might think. Basically, reporters on the beat need to ask better questions and tap the best-informed sources. When journalists accept the challenge of not only reporting what experts say but also questioning what they say, they take a necessary (albeit insufficient) step toward more critical medical reporting.

Listening to experienced medical journalists makes it clear that telling stories that are both true and significant is easier said than done. Not even these basic quality criteria are always met. Journalists constantly face sources who oversell their cases, colleagues who compete for the top story, and media companies who don't hesitate to substitute fiction and entertainment for truth and relevance, in the interest of increasing their market share. Seasoned reporters frown on the "breakthrough-or-alarm" syndrome evidenced by their inexperienced or unscrupulous counterparts. Still, the syndrome is all too common.

What makes medical reporting so intriguing to a journalist is its diversity. Reporting on events ranging from scientific advances and setbacks to fraud and misconduct, from health risks to health promotion, from euthanasia to prevention programs, from population statistics to individuals, from scientific theories to clinical outcomes, from patients' rights to professional concerns, and from public demand to scarce resources makes medical journalism an extraordinarily complex and fascinating field. Medical reporters help inform readers about how to live longer and healthier lives, how to avoid unnecessary suffering, and how to use resources as wisely as possible.

MEDICAL REPORTING MAKES A DIFFERENCE

This book describes common pitfalls in medical reporting and suggests ways to avoid them. The fundamental premise is that medical reporting makes a difference in people's lives. News reports—on a suspected health risk, for instance, or a promising treatment for a common disorder—can convince people to either seek care or steer away from it. Health stories in the media may persuade people to change their lifestyles, as well as contribute to changes in health care practices and policies.[1-4] For example, some doctors knew for a long time that high error rates in the Papanicolaou, or "Pap," test were partly caused by poor laboratory conditions,[5] but it was not until the media highlighted the topic that guidelines were established and error rates declined.[6]

Good reporting can prevent great harm and even save lives. It can empower patients and their families, helping them make informed personal choices and decide when to seek professional care. Investigative medical journalism can expose unacceptable differences in clinical practices and treatment outcomes, report fraud and misconduct, and reveal poor access to health care.

Conversely, bad medical reporting, such as touting unverified health claims, can cause great harm. It can raise unwarranted alarm about alleged health hazards and lead to useless or even harmful reactions. By diverting our attention from what matters and favoring storytelling over scrutiny, bad reporting can undermine our ability to make rational decisions about our own health and to take an active part in the health policy debate. It has been suggested that "poor reporting can mislead and disempower a public that is increasingly affected by science and technology and by decisions determined by technical expertise."[1]

There are many examples of media hype creating false hopes. Timothy Johnson of ABC News has described how a small pilot study concerning an experimental treatment for Alzheimer's disease created "a national media feeding frenzy" in the United States, despite the fact that the study included only four patients, used no control group, relied entirely on subjective outcome assessments by patients' families, and was only single blind (i.e., the doctors knew which treatment the subjects received).[7] Yet, all three commercial networks, as well as many national papers and magazines, reported the results as the emergence of a breakthrough treatment for Alzheimer's disease.[7]

In Italy, a "miracle drug" combination known as the Di Bella multitherapy, effectively promoted by its inventor[8] and extensively covered by journalists as a potential cancer cure,[9–11] garnered so much political support that the courts ruled that Italian hospitals must provide it.[12–13] The hype was created despite the lack of scientific evidence regarding the treatment, and later research suggested that it was not merely ineffective but toxic.[10,13]

Maintaining high standards in medical journalism requires specific knowledge and skills. General reporters who lack special training cannot be expected to have enough insight to ask probing questions, analyze their sources with an eye to finding conflicts of interest, distinguish between news and fads, or frame their stories in a meaningful way. Instead, these reporters are often forced to rely on information that they cannot assess.[14] Not just the news item itself but virtually all the background information is new to them. They have to rely on their sources to judge what is newsworthy and what is not. It's understandable that in such circumstances reporters under a deadline tend to stick to clichés rather than framing the story in a way that puts it in its proper context.[14]

Wittingly or unwittingly, the uninitiated tend to act as megaphones for biased experts, industry, and lobby groups by not placing their claims in an appropriate perspective. Such reporters will uncritically promote new medical treatments, proclaiming them "breakthroughs" even if they are old hat, less effective than existing alternatives, or even worthless, doing patients more harm than good. They will announce "health hazards" and "alarms" without probing for reliable evidence. Meanwhile, they will fail to report the real hazards and miss the effective treatments. And, above all, they will fail to ask the questions that matter most to the audience—is it true, and is it relevant?

"Weather reports, whether in newsprint or on television, have their origins from registered meteorologists. Isn't the public entitled to have science reported by people who have at least been trained in the scientific method?" asks an editorial[15] at the medical Website drkoop.com, commenting on a national media scare about the safety of plastic baby bottles.

At a conference on medicine and the media, involving participants from both fields, it was concluded that "the disproportionate influence of press materials supplied by scientific journals and the sometimes too-cozy relationship between journalists and sources can be alleviated to some extent by journalists' gaining the requisite knowledge and expertise to interpret scientific material accurately and understandably for the public without the assistance of their sources."[16]

SELLING MEDICINE

All too often, health stories in the media are so uncritical that they could just as well have been advertising copy. A case in point is the enthusiastic reporting that an emerging health technology often nets. Before I began writing this book, the front-page headline of an otherwise benign tabloid caught my eye: NEW DIET PILL MAKES YOU BOTH SLIM AND HAPPY. There was nothing extraordinary about the story itself. A new drug was about to be launched. The article simply quoted a few enthusiastic researchers, a moderately impressed clinician, and a patient who had lost weight after treatment— seemingly a straightforward story of scientific progress, like so much other medical reportage.

What was striking about this story, like others of its ilk, was the author's total lack of skepticism. A reporter who fails to ask critical questions or supply the proper context creates an intellectual vacuum that subtly draws the audience into a rose-colored world bearing little resemblance to the real one. In this instance, essentially the same text could have been produced by a copywriter in the manufacturer's marketing department and used as advertising to promote the new product. Shouldn't a more critical approach be expected from a reporter?

Suppose the news item had not been a new diet pill but a new facial cream or the latest car model. Similar headlines might then have read: NEW "MAGIC LIFT" MAKES YOUR SKIN SMOOTH AND ATTRACTIVE or NEW VOLVO MODEL DOES WONDERS FOR YOUR DRIVING. Even if these statements were accurate, such a promotional stance would raise questions. Readers would ask: "Why do they single out this particular product? Is it really superior to any other cream/car? How can they say that, without any evidence to back it up? And if it is true, how does it affect me? Does it mean I should avoid 'Youth Formula' and get rid of my Toyota?" Such flagrant lack of objectivity would probably ignite a storm of letters and e-mail to the editor as well.

In medical news stories, however, individual researchers are often quoted as if they were free from all biases, and such credulity rarely draws fire. As sociology professor Dorothy Nelkin puts it: "Too often science in the press is more a subject for consumption than for public scrutiny, more a source of entertainment than of information. Too often science is presented as an arcane activity outside and above the sphere of normal human understanding, and therefore beyond our control. Too often the coverage is promotional and uncritical, encouraging apathy, a sense of impotence, and the ubiquitous tendency to defer to expertise."[1]

Such problems seem to prevail in the news media at large, not just in its medical wing. A poll of 552 of America's top executives, midlevel editors/producers, and working reporters and editors showed that most journalists and news executives think they are overly focused on internal dynamics, too often competing with each other and writing more for their colleagues than for consumers.[17] Two-thirds of those in national and local news said that news organizations' attempts to attract readers or viewers have pushed them toward "infotainment" instead of news. Growing financial and business pressures were identified as forces driving this overall decline in journalistic quality.

In public debate, the claim that benighted news reports can do real damage is sometimes countered by the argument that there is such a wide variety of news media outlets that many different views will be heard, balancing distorted reporting from any one source. However, research suggests that science journalism is relatively homogeneous: many reports on a given subject focus on the same issues, use the same sources, and interpret the material in similar terms.[18]

Another argument against the impact of uncritical media stories points to the wealth of nonjournalistic sources of up-to-date information. This argument has some empirical support. For example, in 1997, an estimated 30–40 million viewers per week watched the NBC medical drama *ER*.[19] Princeton Survey Research Associates investigated the impact of public health messages conveyed through *ER* in the United States. In a random sample survey of about 1,000 regular *ER* viewers, over half said that they learn about important health care issues from *ER*, and one-third indicated that information they received from the show helped them make choices about their family's health care.[20] As many as 12 percent of viewers reported that they had contacted a physician because of something they had seen on the show.[20]

Furthermore, a vast array of health information is available on the Internet. A survey in the United States showed that nearly half of adult Internet users had recently visited health and medical Websites.[21] At the time of the survey, this figure was estimated to represent some 15.6 million people. One question in this context is whether the abundance of Internet information, of highly varying quality, encourages critical thinking when it comes to media reports. Another issue is whether those who use health care the most have access to the Internet and know how to use it effectively. Moreover, if the public at large, like many reporters, lacks the resources to evaluate medical information, separating the wheat from the chaff, then simply more of the same—whether digital or analog—will not solve the problem.

Lastly, some argue that people who get false or misleading medical information through the media can always see a physician to get the true story. This is only partly accurate. Many clinicians obtain new information, even within their own discipline, from mass-media reports. Two independent surveys from the United States reported that 60 percent of the members of a medical faculty[22] and 90 percent of a sample of private and university physicians[23] said they sometimes acquire professional news through such channels. Even clinicians who manage to keep up with new developments by regularly reading original articles in scientific journals, rather than skimming the news media's digested versions, will often become aware of new developments through the mass media.[24–25]

The theoretical foundation for this book is based mainly on social responsibility theory (as described, e.g., by McQuail)[26] and the journalistic credo specifying the provision of reliable information that is free from distortion, suppression, bias, and sensationalism. Many of the interviews for the book were conducted in the United States, because of its unique position in the global media market, its wide variety of media outlets, and its great diversity of journalistic quality. Much of the literature cited and most of the examples used come from the United States and from media markets that are similar to and/or influenced by the American media—that is, much of the Western world. Medical reporters in different parts of the world outside this sphere may face quite different problems that are not covered here.

Chapter 1 discusses the basic who, what, when, where, and how of medical reporting. Who reports on health and medicine? How are stories selected? What sources are used? How are medical stories reported?

Chapter 2 identifies barriers to critical reporting such as news production routines, limited audience contacts, economic pressures, reliance on sources, and conflicting focuses of interest. It describes how different journalistic approaches toward the same topics can be useful.

Chapter 3 examines the shaky foundations on which medical claims all too often rest, exploring the stakeholders, their vested interests in coverage, and the concept of truth. The chapter also discusses common problems in medical research and how to distinguish between strong and weak scientific evidence; quality criteria for clinical trials and surveys are presented.

Chapter 4 considers how experts can drift from observation to interpretation and then to persuasion and suggests journalistic strategies to get at the truth. Astute reporters explore whether there are alternative ways to interpret findings. Are the experts using rhetoric to make their claims more persuasive? Characteristics of strong and weak argumentation are described, as are classic methods of persuasion. Four reasons to question "promising" treatments are discussed. Different ways to study health care costs are also described.

Chapter 5 presents ten pitfalls in medical reporting. Virtually every journalist on the beat will face these threats to quality medical reporting sooner or later. Recognizing these pitfalls and knowing how to avoid them are key to successful medical reporting.

Chapter 6 explores the concept of critical medical journalism and describes its main features: finding the truth, weighing the evidence, and watching for methodological "red flags." It also discusses related issues such as these: How can systematic reviews of the scientific literature be found and used? What does critical reporting mean to the reporter–source relationship? How does the concept fit with professional standards and journalistic codes of conduct? What about the risk of self-deception among reporters? How can medical reporters deal with scientific uncertainty?

Chapter 7 outlines topics that constantly challenge medical journalists. Special sections deal with health/medical advertising, alternative medicine, and scientific fraud. The chapter ends by outlining issues that judicious medical reporters will explore.

Chapter 8 describes the emerging field of online medical journalism. New media, particularly the Internet and the World Wide Web, open new possibilities for critical medical journalism. The variety of sources and inexpensive online access to some databases offer powerful research tools to medical reporters. However, the new media also raise questions of confidentiality, currency, and accuracy. The chapter briefly covers online public-relations news services, LISTSERVs, newsgroups, medical journal Websites, e-interviews, and several general points regarding online publishing.

The glossary at the back of the book covers many of the terms and concepts frequently used (and abused) by sources and reporters on the medical beat.

To recap, this book focuses on the critical potential of medical reporting. I have therefore studied the works of leading medical reporters—outstanding professionals who are among the best in their field. Many have long careers behind them, and some enjoy exceptional professional freedom and have access to considerable resources. Under less favorable working conditions, some of the pitfalls they describe may be hard to avoid, and some of the goals hard to reach. Nevertheless, much can be learned from their experience, information that can be invaluable even in very different settings.

If good medical journalism reaches a large audience—whether in print, broadcast, or electronic format—then perhaps this audience will find itself in a better position to judge what is probably true, what is uncertain, and what is probably junk.

Acknowledgments

I would like to thank all those who have made this book possible. I am particularly indebted to Andrew Skolnick, Dorothy Nelkin of New York University, Lawrence K. Altman and Nicholas Wade of the *New York Times,* Rebecca Perl and Richard Harris of National Public Radio, Deborah Blum of the University of Wisconsin—Madison, Brian McCormick of *American Medical News,* Tom Rosenstiel of the Project for Excellence in Journalism, Howard Lewis of the National Association of Science Writers, Bruce Dan of Medcast Networks, and the following editors at the *Journal of the American Medical Association:* Annette Flanagin, Phil Fontanarosa, Margaret Winker, Richard Glass, and Mike Mitka.

My dear father, Dr. Lennart Levi, who has devoted his career to scientific research and to getting the findings into health policy and practice, and my longtime friend Katti Björklund, student of journalism at Stockholm University, gave valuable feedback. So did Dr. Andrew Herxheimer of the U.K. Cochrane Centre, Christina Bergh, who kindly reviewed philosophical aspects of the text, and Dr. Jörgen Malmquist, who offered useful advice regarding some statistical issues. Serena Stockwell made interesting remarks based on her experiences as the editor of *Oncology Times.* Robbie Wallin and Ron Gustafson generously shared their deep knowledge of language and style. I would also like to thank many colleagues in the Swedish Association of Medical Writers for years of stimulating discussions, and British consumer activist David Gilbert for sharing his thoughts on the role of medical journalism.

In addition, I have met with a number of experienced people who work, not for the media, but on "the other side of the fence," that is, professionals in public relations and communications. The following communicators have been particularly helpful: Debbie Rosenberg Bush and Avice Meehan of Memorial Sloan-Kettering Cancer Center, Mark Stuart of Hill and Knowlton, and Dorothy Oliver Pirovano of Public Communications, Inc. They have all discussed with me their observations about the road from science, through public-relations agencies, into the media.

Financial support was provided by grants from The Swedish Institute and The Lars Salvius Foundation. I would also like to thank Kjersti Board, Consulate General of Sweden, and Lena Daun, Swedish Institute, for their assistance with the logistics of a study trip to the United States.

Last, but not least, I want to thank my family for tolerating all my late nights and early mornings of writing, for believing in the idea of writing this book, and for being wonderfully supportive.

Ragnar Levi

Medical Journalism

CHAPTER 1

The Media Meet Medicine

Be careful about reading health books. You may die of a misprint.
—Mark Twain (1835–1910)

Believe nothing you see in the newspapers. They have done more to create dissatisfaction than all other agencies. If you see anything in them that you know is true, begin to doubt it at once.
—Sir William Osler (1849–1919)

Chapter objectives
- **Discuss the importance of medical journalism**
- **Examine the process of medical reporting**

WHAT IS MEDICAL JOURNALISM?

Few media topics are as exciting and diversified as health and medicine. The field has treats for almost every taste. It deals with life and death, hope and fear, health and disease, progress and failure, coping and crises, fact and speculation, safety and risks. Medical reporters deal with everything from the highest technology to the helping hand, from laboratory science to hands-on clinical practice.

Medical scientists' quest for knowledge and their constant fight for funding spawn stories of fame and fortune, as well as investigative series on failure and fraud. Insurance organizations and the health industry represent powerful commercial interests that reporters watch, always on the alert for abuse of power or injustice. At times, hospitals, clinics, and health professionals fail to deliver good medical care to everyone who has a right to it. Medical reporters have to deal not only with the scientific, political, economic, and ethical aspects of medicine but also with human-interest stories of individual patients and health professionals fighting against disease and suffering. Health stories cover the spectrum from highly emotional, even sentimental, to rational and thought-provoking. In short, medical reporting is a thrill.

It is therefore not surprising that health stories attract a large audience, as evidenced by many surveys. For example, a 1993 Gallup poll of 1,017 respondents asked whether the media gave enough attention to health and medical issues.[27] The largest single category of respondents (35 percent) said they would like to see "a lot more."

Only 6 percent said they would like to see "a little less" or "a lot less." Scientific studies suggest that not only the general public but even health care professionals and policymakers get much of their information about health from reports by professional journalists.[28-33]

All this information not only influences awareness, attitudes, and intentions but may also contribute to changes in behavior, health care utilization, clinical practices, and health policies.[34] Although research on health reports' impact on behavior is fairly limited, many examples of drastic behavior changes have been described. When the media reported that dietary studies showed a connection between cholesterol-producing foods and heart disease, the consumption of beef, eggs, and fatty milk products dropped.[1] Sales of salt-free products boomed in the wake of reports on the risks of excessive sodium intake. The national scare in the United States in 1989 caused by press reports on the cancer-causing pesticide Alar being sprayed on apples was described as follows in a *Washington Post* editorial on June 1, 1997: "A complicated scientific issue was allowed to be decided not by officials charged with protecting the public, on the basis of hard evidence, but by a frightened public acting on incomplete and often erroneous press reports."

Media reports may influence what conditions are perceived as health problems requiring professional consultation and care. A systematic review of the best available scientific evidence in the field found that mass-media reports have a statistically significant and important impact on health services utilization.[35]

By featuring certain topics and excluding others, and choosing how to frame stories, the news media seem to not only reflect the public debate but also play an important part in setting the agenda, affecting public demand, and influencing the allocation of resources. In this respect, medical reporting is political. According to Pulitzer Prize–winning science reporter Deborah Blum, previously at the *Sacramento Bee* and now at the University of Wisconsin, the political aspects are not always obvious: "You can go into medical journalism thinking 'I am not going to be a political reporter' only to find out that few topics are more political."[36]

For the purposes of this book, medical journalism is defined broadly as professional journalists' reporting of health and medical stories and health-related topics in the mass media. The focus here is mainly on scientific issues and how these can be best covered. Common health-related topics include new methods for diagnosis and treatment; health risks related to diet, sedentary lifestyle, and genetic factors; access to health care; and issues related to the organization and funding of health care.

Articles written by scientists for publication in medical journals lie outside the scope of medical journalism. As a rule, such articles are not written by journalists and do not meet journalistic criteria for form and content.

Generally, medical journalism, as defined here, targets the public at large rather than specific professional groups within the clinical professions or health administration. As noted earlier, however, even these groups follow media reports closely. According to two independent surveys in the United States, 60 percent of members of a medical faculty[37] and nearly 90 percent of a sample of university and private physicians[23] said that they sometimes get professional news through the mass media.

Considering the marked public interest in health/medical stories, it is not surprising that so many topics and actors within health care, medical science, and the drug and device industry compete for media attention.

WHO DOES IT AND WHERE?

Many medical news stories are told by reporters without any particular training in, or knowledge of, health issues. They are not specialized medical or science journalists. For example, in the United States, only about 10 percent of the 1,650 daily newspapers employed science writers in the mid-1980s.[38] In 1996, Tom Wilkie, science editor of the *Independent*, noted that only eight full-time employees worked as health/medical reporters in national daily broadsheet newspapers in Great Britain, while another eight covered the whole range of science issues, including information technology and environmental topics.[39] By contrast, the *New York Times* alone employed nine staff writers and four editors in science.[39]

Commenting on the British situation, Wilkie notes: "Such a small number of people face obvious logistical difficulties simply in covering news events as they happen, without the problems of trying to develop deeper expertise in any particular topic or to carry out 'investigative' reporting."[39]

Studies from the 1960s and 1970s suggest that not even reporters who specialize in science seem satisfied with their skills in this field but usually recommend that science journalists get more training.[40–41] Limited data from a more recent Swedish survey[42] indicate that many medical reporters still lack special training.

In many media, general reporters cover not only politics, crime, wars, disasters, business, and national budget issues. They are also expected to report on everything from the latest findings in genetic research and molecular biology to what new drugs are good for, how infectious diseases spread, and when women should be screened for breast cancer. Television and radio reporters are particularly likely to be generalists,[43] whereas some wire services providing medical news have experienced staff science writers.

Some argue that general reporters are less likely to be biased and therefore are better equipped to report medical news than special health reporters who identify with their beat. True, specialized reporters need to recognize the risk of getting too "cozy" with their sources and need to maintain a professional distance. However, this is a poor excuse for underestimating the value of special skills and experience. The advantage of having sufficient knowledge of a complex field like medicine to tell truths from half-truths or outright lies outweighs the potential drawbacks. However, some data from the United States suggest that newspaper editors may be unwilling to pay for additional training of reporters who cover medicine.[44]

Although general reporters may be able to draw on their experiences from other fields to investigate health/medical topics, thus giving their stories a different slant, many find it difficult to evaluate potential news items and to ask critical questions. Nevertheless, a great many breaking general news stories may have a scientific or technical component that a general reporter may be forced to handle. Even general reporters need at least a basic understanding of the pitfalls of medical reporting.

A Swedish study from 1992 found that specialized reporters constitute only one-third of 1,240 news reporters studied at daily newspapers, tabloids, regional/local newspapers, national and local radio stations, and television news desks[14] although the percentage varies considerably among the different types of media.

Even when the media do employ special health reporters, they are not always allowed to focus exclusively on their field. Of almost 2,000 journalistic assignments studied on one day in Sweden, only one in seven was carried out by a reporter specialized in the field in question.[14]

Considering the complexity of many medical topics, and the fast pace of technological change in health care, it is not surprising that some stories are characterized by poor framing and misconceptions.

Journalists report health stories in different media, including newspapers, magazines, newsletters, radio, television, the Internet, and electronic news and feature services. These media vary greatly with respect to audience, function, content and form, frequency and reach, production process, financing, and ownership.[26]

Consider, for example, the differences between medical stories in various print media, such as the national press (on news pages, health pages, women's pages, other feature pages, editorials, and color supplements), local press (on news pages), popular scientific journals, consumer magazines, special-interest magazines, and newsletters. Radio and television broadcasters vary a health story's slant, depending on whether the context is a network news program, a local news program, a special program, or a documentary. A photogenic news peg, with exciting graphics and footage, is likely to be considered more newsworthy by a television team. Radio coverage of medical news may have different profiles at commercial and public-service radio stations/networks. Complicated medical stories often have a greater chance of being covered by public-service radio than by commercial radio stations, many of which prefer medical news that fits into a forty-second sound bite.

Some of the material in print and broadcast media originates from electronic news and feature services, such as Reuters, Associated Press (AP), and United Press International (UPI). Some media syndicates offer their subscribers medical stories written by special health or science reporters. Three large news services are truly global: Reuters, AP, and Agence France-Press (AFP). In recent decades, global news-film agencies have emerged, including Visnews (with stakeholders like Reuters and BBC), Associated Press Television News (APTN), CBS, and Cable News Network (CNN). The market has been characterized by vertical and horizontal integration of these agencies, as well as conglomerate mergers,[45] illustrated by the historic mega-merger between

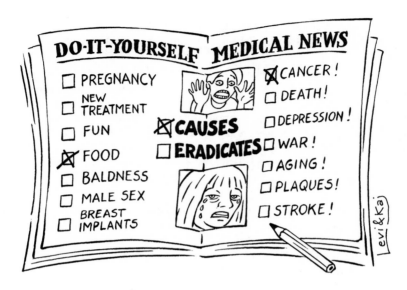

the world's largest Internet gateway America Online and the media giant Time Warner in January 2000.

WHAT ISSUES ARE COVERED?

Medical news can be events, opinions, or facts. Media workers have to sift a vast amount of information every day, choosing what to report and what not to. Only a small fraction of all potentially newsworthy medical issues are actually reported. This may cause considerable frustration among sources who feel that the media give a distorted view of the world and/or that important messages are being neglected. Journalists, on the other hand, defend their decisions by arguing that their mission is to be critical and selective and to simplify complicated issues.

What is interesting about these arguments is that both the sources and the media workers refer to what the audience wants or needs. Yet, they have completely different views of what that actually is. Both parties may be setting their priorities on the basis of their own assumptions and prejudices rather than on relevant background information or actual feedback from the public. Crude consumption patterns are a poor substitute for systematic and detailed audience feedback.

Nevertheless, editors and journalists must every day make choices based on their professional judgment of a story's newsworthiness and their assumptions about the audience. For example, research suggests that medicine in the media tends to focus on hospital-based medicine and pay scant attention to social explanations of ill health.[46-47] Critics have suggested that some of the most important medical issues are not covered by the press.[48]

Media researchers have suggested that a number of general criteria are used, implicitly or explicitly, by the media industry in the selection process. By analyzing the stories as they are told in the media, and by participatory observations of the selection process, researchers have tried to pinpoint different aspects of news value. Important factors influencing news value were described as early as the 1960s by researchers like Johan Galtung and Mari Ruge. They identified the following qualities, which may act as signals to news audiences and help media workers quickly sort through, process, and select the news:[49-50]

- *Short time span:* Events that unfold and acquire meaning quickly and that fit into the media's daily production routine are preferable to long-term processes.
- *Scale* and *intensity:* Any event must pass a certain threshold before it will be recorded at all. An issue perceived as more significant than other issues is obviously more likely to get reported, and this perception is influenced by previous media coverage.
- *Clarity:* Clear and unequivocal issues are more likely to be covered than those that are ambiguous or less obviously good or bad.
- *Meaningfulness:* Cultural proximity and relevance are the criteria that rule here. The familiar and culturally similar will get particular attention. On the other hand, a conflict with distant cultures may attract attention even to the latter.
- *Consonance:* The media prefer stories that reinforce society's existing expectations. If there is public demand for a certain event, and this event has been anticipated, the likelihood is greater that it will be reported.
- *Unexpectedness:* Within the set of the meaningful and the consonant, unusual and surprising events have the highest chances of becoming news.
- *Continuity:* Once something has made headlines, it will continue to be defined as news for some time, even if the coverage is drastically reduced.
- *Composition:* An issue that fits into the balance among different categories— the desirable news mix—will have a greater chance of being reported. Conversely, if there are already many medical news items, the threshold for a new item will be higher.
- *Reference to elites:* Most news refers to elite persons or elite nations. Ordinary people are often represented by proxy, that is, by authorities or experts.
- *Personification:* News that can be reported as human stories eliciting empathy or disapproval is preferable to abstract, impersonal items.
- *Negativity:* Bad news tends to get more coverage than good news.

According to communications researcher Henk Prakke,[51] the concept of news value can be described in three dimensions (popular interpretations in parentheses):

No, Dr. Wheeler, this is a news show. You can't say hello to the Nobel Prize Committee on air.

(1) time distance ("is," "was," or "has been"), (2) cultural distance ("engaged," "interested," or "aware"), and (3) spatial distance ("here," "near," or "there"). In other words, issues perceived as being current and close and affecting the audience will receive more attention.[52]

Other researchers have stressed the media's general preference for elite persons as sources—a preference that is even stronger in the context of science news. The technical nature of this type of news encourages reliance on official sources of information who know how to package information for the press.[1] These sources do not necessarily represent a wide spectrum of opinion.

The factors that make for newsworthiness will be interpreted differently by different people in different settings. Judgments about which events are new, significant, unexpected, or meaningful will obviously be influenced by media workers' knowledge, personal experience, and cultural and ideological framework.

Many stories that meet the criteria for news value never see the light of day, while others with far less news value get published. One reason is space. There are pages to fill in daily newspapers and airtime to fill in broadcasts. Editorial judgments about the value of particular news items is naturally influenced by how many other important stories are breaking at the same time. A plane crash might rule out a story of a new cancer treatment, while a marginal medical event may be a top story on a slow news day.[53]

WHAT SOURCES ARE USED?

Medical journals are important sources for health reporters, providing a wealth of information and story ideas.[54] In a study of five Dutch newspapers, 45 of 178 newspaper articles on pharmaceuticals were based on reports in medical and scientific journals.[55] Journals are also increasingly active in promoting their own material. Many have built formidable publicity machines employing public-relations and marketing departments to ensure that their articles will be widely quoted, attracting more readers and advertisers.

These journals too, like other media, are of course commercial enterprises. Two major medical journals, the *New England Journal of Medicine* and *Journal of the American Medical Association (JAMA)*, have display advertising revenues in the $20–25 million range (1997), of which the vast bulk comes from pharmaceutical companies.[56-57]

While papers in peer-reviewed scientific journals are often expected to be more reliable than nonreviewed, unpublished data, blind faith in such journals may cause problems. In some infamous cases, editorials that appeared to have been written by independent physicians had in fact been commissioned, paid for, and partly written by public-relations firms that represented drug companies.[58-60]

Furthermore, only part of the truth is told in peer-reviewed journals. It is well known that publication of articles in scientific medical journals is key in the biomedical industry's marketing strategy. Companies may select journals in which study results pertaining to their products will appear, pick the scientists they know will have access to these journals, and use the published articles to market their products. Economic incentives encourage researchers to design studies that are likely to show desirable results, and to omit publication of "negative findings," that is, studies that demonstrate no significant difference between various treatments. As one researcher frankly put it: "Who wants to perform a randomized trial to show that what you're developing doesn't help people?"

Scientific medical literature is skewed by publication bias. For example, research shows that articles demonstrating that a treatment works well are more likely to be published than those that report uncertain results or show that a treatment has no useful effect.[61] Scientists are less likely to submit such studies for publication,[61] and medical journals are less likely to publish them.[62] Some research findings suggest that the news media reinforce this bias. A comparison of newspaper coverage of two studies analyzing radiation as a cancer risk (published back-to-back in the March 20, 1991, issue of *JAMA*) found that the study showing adverse effects received better media coverage than the study that did not. In terms of the number, length, and quality of newspaper reports, the study showing adverse effects netted far better coverage than the other study.[63]

When researchers want to publish studies that do not show a desired effect, or that report results unfavorable to particular drugs or devices, the industry may pressure them not to do so. More specifically, the tobacco, pharmaceutical, and medical-device industries have been accused of using intimidation and lawsuits to prevent or delay the publication of research they consider damaging.[64-65]

Suppression of unfavorable research findings was discussed at a Cantigny Conference titled "Ethical Issues in the Publication of Medical Information." At this conference, Drummond Rennie, adjunct professor of medicine at the University of California–San Francisco and deputy editor (West) of *JAMA,* described how a major pharmaceutical company launched an intensive campaign to discredit the authors and results of a study that was unfavorable to their product, an artificial hormone. According to Rennie, this company lodged "about four dozen specific complaints about the study and all sorts of accusations of unethical conduct on the part of the authors."[53] He said one of the authors phoned him two weeks before the planned publication to say that they were withdrawing the paper because the senior author had twice been threatened with legal action if the company suffered any bad consequences. While the senior author confirmed this, the makers of the product denied it, said Rennie.[63] Most descriptions of publication bias are not so blatant.

Indeed, many studies published in peer-reviewed journals are flawed and therefore unreliable. Their results make sense only when viewed in the context of previous findings, and only when each study's shortcomings are taken into account. However, few journalists have had the training necessary to interpret findings in a relevant context, to question research results, or to challenge interpretations and extrapolations of these results by experts. The resulting media reports may therefore fail to clarify the implications of the results[66]—or, in the worst cases, further muddy the water.

Medical reporter Andrew Skolnick comments: "Many health journalists, particularly TV reporters, simply rewrite press releases from medical journals. They make a phone call to talk for ten minutes with the principal investigator, take some quotes, and then think they have done their job. They have not."[67]

Rebecca Perl of National Public Radio says: "It is not always good enough that a study has been published by a reputable medical journal. A lot of the journals also want to sell and get their name out there. I feel the bar has to be set very high for medical stories. It is very important that we reporters are able to judge the quality of a study. We need to know a little bit of statistics, and we need to be able to ask hard questions."[68]

Peer-reviewed journals are certainly not the only source for medical stories. Media reports may also originate from scientific meetings and similar events, press conferences and press releases, tip-offs from colleagues and other media reports, experts, public-information officers, patients, and other individual stakeholders.[69] Here, similar problems may arise. So-called public-relations news wires on the Internet are a case in point, feeding the media with corporate-sponsored material. (Some of the special problems related to using material from the World Wide Web are outlined in chapter 8.) Sarah Masters, vice president and editor-in-chief of Reuters Health Information, pinpoints why reporters should be wary when tapping such wire services: "These are not news wires; they are simply a way to convey press releases that are corporate-sponsored to the news media in a new way. But quite a number of services, including Reuters, though not Reuters Health, run them as is, so that what appears on Reuters' news wires can easily be mistaken for researched content rather than as a straight, flat-out press release."[63]

It has been suugested that inexperienced writers are the most likely to rely on press conferences and to passively accept the material provided, instead of actively pursuing the stories.

Experts are frequently used by journalists as a primary information source. Quoting experts is a popular narrative technique in the lay media. While some experts are easily accessible, seemingly authoritative, and willing to help reporters understand complicated issues, many others are not. The most communicative experts are not necessarily the most knowledgeable and reliable:

> Less sophisticated reporters will often turn for expertise to those scientists who happen to be most accessible, often those teaching in a local university. Usually the reporter cannot assess the experience of these scientists, their knowledge of the subject, or their reliability as sources. Faced with technical terms that are difficult to check out, and socialized to regard scientists as a reliable and objective source of information, these journalists are inclined to believe what they are told.[1]

When reporters want to bolster their stories with comments from the scientific community, they seek out experts who can speak with enthusiasm about the results and who have previously contributed lively comments.[70] Chances are, however, that such experts will present their personal opinions rather than summarizing and commenting on the best available scientific evidence.

For example, the authors of a structured evaluation of thirty health-related articles published in five Norwegian daily newspapers during one week concluded that it was generally impossible to distinguish opinions from facts or to assess the validity and consistency of the underlying evidence.[71] Most articles failed to provide sufficient analysis, and some went so far off course as to focus on medical curiosities and alleged miracles.

Industry may exaggerate favorable findings in press releases following the publication of scientific papers, pushing conclusions far beyond what the data can support. The reasons are obvious. It has been documented that media coverage of scientific findings can affect stock values. For example, some observations suggest that an article about a particular product on the front page of a prestigious newspaper can influence the parent company's stock value even in the absence of published data regarding the product's effectiveness.[53] This has led some scientists to consider possible stock market responses before making their results public.[72]

The drug and device industries are not alone in hungering for timely media attention. According to Kristina Gunsalus, associate provost of the University of Illinois, universities, being in need of the resources offered by corporations, are increasingly regarded as representing a special interest.[53] This is confirmed by Dorothy Pirovano, senior vice president of Public Communications, Inc., a public-relations company that services its wide variety of clients from the medical field by deploying such tools as prerecorded feature stories (radio actualities), video news releases, television news film bites (b-roll), and live satellite interviews on breaking stories. Pirovano comments: "Everybody has their reasons to be hungry for publicity—not only pharmaceutical companies and device manufacturers, but also hospitals, clinics, medical schools, and insurance companies. They all more or less want to drive business in a particular way. There is always that pragmatic side. What most of them ask us to do is to generate stories in the press—that is the backbone of our activities."[73]

Some sources hire public-relations firms with expertise in catering to the interests of individual reporters. "The trick is to tease reporters' needs and interests and to build relationships with them," explains Mark Stuart, a senior public-relations director who has worked at Hill and Knowlton, a major international public-relations firm that boasts pharmaceutical corporations among its clients.

> I quickly learned to drop the classic who, what, when, where, and why. That's not what reporters want. They want to tell good stories. So they need human faces, people, the picture, the family portrait. A slice of life, if you will. That's the kind of emotional trigger reporters need. Either they'll see their own aunt or uncle in these patients, or they'll identify with them. I've learned that if they do that, they will buy the story and help sell it to their bosses. But you have to get to know every reporter to know what buttons to push. Unfortunately, many still don't realize how useful we PR people are.[74]

Although information provided by public-relations officials may on occasion be useful, critical reporters realize that such information is likely to be biased. The official guide of the U.S. National Association of Science Writers warns its members to be wary of possible bias in press announcements and unsolicited tips from public-relations people and unknown scientists. Funding, competition, ambition, and the desire for glory may color their agendas.[69]

In summary, journalists often get too little of the information they really need and too much of biased, incomplete, and/or irrelevant information.[53] Although reporters are generally skeptical toward public-relations officers, the mutual dependence between sources and media workers can influence medical reporting. Peter Garpenby, journalist and health services researcher at the Center for Medical Technology at Linköping University in Sweden, comments: "There is a kind of gamesmanship between the sources and the mass media. Sources are interested in bringing attention to certain issues. The media chooses the subjects and the angles, which in turn influences how the topic is approached later."[75]

Avice Meehan, vice president of public affairs at Memorial Sloan-Kettering Cancer Center in New York, expresses a similar view: "The reporter has something we want, that is, access to readers and viewers. We have something that they may want—a story. That's where the dance comes in."[76]

Despite frequent invitations to "dance," working relationships between medical reporters and their sources can at times be strained. However, such tensions may mainly grow out of disagreement about the role of the media, perceived differences in defining science news, and conflicts over styles of reporting.[77] For example, while replication of research results and endorsement by colleagues are important to scientists, journalists are more interested in fresh or dramatic research findings, even if they are tentative. To reporters, established ideas may sound like "old news."

HOW ARE STORIES TOLD?

Many journalists liken their professional role to a mirror that reflects reality in an objective fashion. However, as attractive as such an ideal image may be to the reporter, the metaphor of a mirror is misleading. Science reporter Deborah Blum says: "Objectivity in journalism is a myth. Even if I include all different points of view in my stories, I am still going to make subjective decisions on whom I choose to interview, where I will let them appear in the piece, which of the quotes I am going to use, and how I am going to frame the story."[36]

Skilled journalists do not simply spew out in their reports all the information they have gathered, acting as a passive megaphone, but instead are selective and critical. This means not taking information at face value but exploring on what grounds and for what reasons a particular source makes a claim. It also means examining the source's context: what group or organization is making the claim, from what perspective, and who benefits? In so doing, journalists "impose coherence on an otherwise chaotic form of events," as journalism scholar James Carey has noted.

Being a watchdog, a critical observer, means recognizing that all knowledge presumes some point of view, including the reporter's own. The idea of a completely objective reporter (or, for that matter, source) is absurd, since the whole working process—including the selection of news items, the choice of a journalistic angle, and the use of a narrative technique—constitutes a series of personal standpoints. The decisions required involve judgment, interpretations, and sometimes speculation, all of which reflect the varying interests, knowledge levels, and professional skills of media workers. Thus, opponents to the mirror metaphor have compared science writers to brokers who frame social reality for their audience and shape public consciousness about science-related events.[1]

Journalists pursuing a story use their professional skills and judgment to tease out a news peg on which the rest of the story can be hung. Most news reports start with the most interesting point and work their way toward the least interesting. The stories are expected to provide answers to at least five basic questions that all reporters are taught: Who? What? When? Where? How? In addition, they may address the important but more complicated question of Why? Since most news reports are expected to be brief, the last question is often neglected (though feature articles and special programs may deal with this aspect at length).

The Poynter Institute, a reputable U.S.-based school for journalists and journalism teachers, has outlined the skills a reporter must acquire to use language effectively:[78]

- Master the news narrative's elements, from the challenge of summing up a story in a sentence or a paragraph to painting a scene with words that evoke a response.
- Organize complex elements into a coherent whole.
- Create language that clarifies and complements but does not compete with content.
- Integrate other story dimensions, such as sound and video, with the written word.
- Serve as the bridge to professions and politicians, translating jargon or complex verbiage into clear language.
- Avoid errors in spelling, grammar, vocabulary, and punctuation so as not to distract or confuse the audience.

How is front-page news framed by the media? The U.S. Project for Excellence in Journalism (PEJ, a program run by the Columbia University Graduate School of Journalism and underwritten by the Pew Charitable Trusts) and Princeton Survey Research Associates have identified a number of potential narrative frames:[79]

- *Straight news account*—no dominant frame other than outlining the basic who, what, when, where, why, and how
- *Conflict story*—a focus on conflict inherent in the situation or brewing among the players
- *Consensus story*—an emphasis on the points of agreement around an issue or event
- *Conjecture story*—a focus on speculation about what is to come
- *Process story*—an explanation of how a process unfolds or how something works
- *Historical outlook*—how the current news fits into history
- *Horse race*—who is winning and who is losing
- *Trend story*—the news as an ongoing trend
- *Policy explored*—a focus on exploring policy and its impact
- *Reaction story*—a response or reaction to a previous event from one of the major players
- *Reality check*—a close look into the veracity of a statement made or information given
- *Wrongdoing exposed*—the uncovering of faults, crimes, or injustice
- *Personality profile*—a profile of the newsmaker

The PEJ researchers have conducted a two-month-long pilot study in which they examined the front-page news offered by seven American newspapers—three national papers and four regional ones. The data they gathered will be used in a larger study, but their preliminary hypothesis is that newspapers employ a variety of frames, at least on their front pages, and no one frame dominates.[79] Although medical journalism was not specifically explored in this study, such reporting probably employs most of these frames, to a greater or lesser extent.

But journalists must be careful not to force a medical story into a frame that does not fit it. Critics claim that a fundamental problem in media reports about medical science is that journalists construct "events," making science look like a series of breakthroughs instead of the slow and laborious process that it usually is.

Fundamentally, the journalistic method of telling stories is concisely described by five imperatives: clarify, simplify, polarize, intensify, and personify. Journalists must break down complicated issues into a few digestible pieces. For the sake of simplicity and clarity, they must leave out many details. For the same reason, but also for the sake of drama, they may personify opinions and play conflicting values against each other. They may highlight and amplify particularly newsworthy issues. And, finally, they usually make abstract discussions concrete by using examples that the audience will readily recognize.

At times, journalists go too far, and the stakes are high. Speaking at a medical reporters' seminar entitled "The Need for Critical Reporting," David Gilbert, consumer activist at King's Fund in London, commented: "It is us, the readers, who suffer from uncritical, sensationalist, oversimplified and polarizing stories. They reduce journalism to entertainment, while facts and criticism of the sources come second."[80] Gilbert went on to question the lack of critical and investigative thinking in medical reporting and the abundance of stereotyped and narrow coverage of issues. "Too little attention is paid to the questions consumers ask," he said, referring to questions such as those listed in table 2.1.

Not only stakeholders in the audience but also journalists and editors have been quite harsh in their critique of news reporting as it is today. For example, in a 1998–99 Pew Research Center survey of 552 top U.S. executives, midlevel editors/producers, and working reporters and editors, a majority of respondents agreed that the lines have blurred between commentary and reporting, and between entertainment and news.[17] According to the same survey, a growing number of reporters, editors, and news executives also agreed that news reports are full of factual errors and sloppy reporting.[17]

Science writer Deborah Blum says: "American television, with few exceptions, is the wasteland of medical reporting. It is 'rah-rah' and 'gee-whiz' about most things. They broadcast canned video news releases from universities and what-not, and it is total PR. And, I am sorry to say, most science reporting programs at universities in this country focus on print journalism, not television."[36]

However, it is not only television that incites critics' ire. In their introduction to an anthology of science writing, science writers and editors Ted Anton and Rick McCourt remark: "The general fare in journalism, even in the most august science section of all, Tuesday's *New York Times,* is often uneven, overhyped, and occasionally downright wrong." They continue: "The errors can include the sensationalism of taking the latest from the *New England Journal of Medicine* and dressing it up the day it's published—sometimes prepackaged by a scientist or institutional press office. . . . The most common error in science writing is to overblow the 'breakthrough' of a new discovery."[81]

For example, in the mid-1990s, an optimistic *Newsweek* cover story on the hormone melatonin,[82] along with overwhelmingly positive reports in other media about the "anti-aging drug," spurred a public demand that ran far ahead of the scientific evidence regarding the hormone's anti-aging effects. At the time, a major manufacturer estimated that 20 million new American melatonin consumers were added in the course of one year.[83] Furthermore, critics pointed out that one of the sources being quoted about the alleged anti-aging properties of melatonin had also written a popular book on the topic and stood to gain personally from the press attention. Nevertheless, media reports had described this man only as "a scientist," failing to disclose his potential source of bias.[84]

CHAPTER 2

Barriers to Serving the Audience

You'd better do what you feel good about doing. If we [try to] figure out what it is the audience wants and then try to deliver it to them, we're lost souls on the ghost ship forever.

—Dan Rather (1931–)

The reporter is the daily prisoner of clocked facts. . . . On all working days, he is expected to do his best in one swift swipe at each story.

—Jim Bishop (1907–87)

Chapter objectives
- **Describe potential barriers to good reporting**
- **Outline different journalistic styles**

News media generally claim to meet their audiences' needs and interests. More specifically, many journalists take pride in scrutinizing those in power, forming what is often called the Fourth Estate. Some even promise to present events in an objective fashion, while others recognize their own subjective role in the newsmaking process. Regardless, media workers claim to represent their audiences' interests. Many news reporters see themselves as the public's advocate and feel that they have a mission to tell their stories with the reader's interest as their guiding star.

However, many practical obstacles stand in the way of these ideals—particularly in a complex field like medicine. Five of the most common obstacles—news production routines, limited contact with the audiences, economic pressures, reliance on sources, and conflicting focuses of interest—are worth examining closely.

NEWS PRODUCTION ROUTINES

The media industry imposes the constraints of time pressure, brevity, and simplicity on all its employees. Working conditions and competition for "breaking news" push media workers to speed up the reporting process as much as possible. Medical reporters often complain that they have no time to check experts' claims. Limitations in page space or time on air may demand cutting stories to the bone and further. A quest to simplify complicated medical stories may also stand in the way of analyzing and qualifying expert statements or putting them in a larger context. Many scientists and clinicians lack training in communicating with journalists and have little understanding for their deadlines.

The standard deadlines that drive the media industry can be quite rigid. Rather than responding to the complexity of each individual news item and determining the time and other resources necessary to complete every assignment in a meaningful way, reporters may feel compelled to let routine deadlines set the limits.[14] Thus, they may not have the necessary resources for them to sort out the extent and significance of a medical problem, or its causes, potential harm, possible treatment, or prevention— even when such information would be of great interest to their readers.

After journalists hand in their reports, other media professionals take over. Editors, subeditors, and headline writers with less insight concerning the topics reported will go over the stories; decide whether to publish them; and then copyedit and shorten the ones to be published, providing them with introductions, leads, and headlines that may or may not reflect the content; and, finally, put them in a more or less prominent place in the final media product. These judgments are usually made without consulting the reporter. Editors and reporters may differ in their views of what criteria should be used in this process. In one study of editorial judgment, editors evaluated news stories primarily on the basis of their interest and excitement, whereas science writers based their evaluations more on accuracy and significance.[85]

LIMITED AUDIENCE CONTACT

Meeting readers', listeners', and viewers' specific needs and interests may be a problem for journalists who have limited contact with their audiences—which is often the case.[17,86-88] In fact, few journalists and editors ever receive systematic feedback from their audiences.[45,1] Their view of readers', listeners', and viewers' interests may be based on a combination of scattered reader contacts, crude audience statistics, and guesswork.

Science journalists and editors operate on a set of assumptions about their audiences that influences their reporting, including the selection, style, and format of stories.[1] These assumptions may be reinforced by other media workers. Many journalists are in daily contact with their peers and function as each other's reference group.[45]

What do audiences really want? Little research is available concerning audiences' specific expectations on medical reports in the media. More research efforts have been dedicated to investigating consumer demands on patient information in general, and their findings may provide guidance for medical writers. For example, one study focusing on what questions are most frequently asked by patients with common health problems identified several important issues,[89] some of which are summarized in table 2.1.

Currently, the Internet seems to be improving contacts between media workers and parts of their audiences. Some medical reporters receive audience feedback via e-mail on a regular basis and use it as a starting point for future stories. Chat groups

Table 2.1.   Important issues from a patient's perspective
(adapted from Coulter et al. 1999)[89]

A. Health problem
What is causing the problem?
How does my experience compare with that of other patients?
What can I, as a patient, do to ameliorate the problem?
How does this problem affect my risk for disease in the future?
What is the purpose of the tests and examinations?
B. Treatment
Is it necessary to be treated for this problem?
What are the different options?
What are the treatment benefits from each of these options?
Will treatment relieve the symptoms?
What are the risks/side effects? Effects on emotions? On everyday life? On sex life?
How can I prepare for treatment?
Where can I find more information?
C. Recovery
How long does it take to recover?
What can I do to speed recovery?
What are the options for rehabilitation?
How can I prevent future recurrence of illness?

and Net meetings are set up by some media to enhance audience interaction, especially if they have just covered controversial issues or events.

ECONOMIC PRESSURES

Jerry Bishop, editor and medical reporter for the *Wall Street Journal,* has noted: "I am responsible to the owners of The Wall Street Journal to do what they set out to do— to operate to make money. To make a profit—that's what my job is. They've told me, 'We want you to keep an eye on what's going on in science and in medicine. You go out and find out what is of interest to our readers in this field. We will publish it. The readers will buy it and we'll make a little money.'"[16]

The industry-like nature of the news production system has been recognized by media researchers.[90–91] Such key features of industrial production as fragmenting the production process, using cut-and-dried working methods, rationalizing to increase productivity, and using easily replaceable workers apply to many news media organizations.[14]

*Your story is great, but it's still not sexy enough for page one. Go find out if
Madonna has been treated.*

Like any industry, the largely market-driven media industry is intent on maximizing profits. Potential sources of media income are advertising, subscriptions, and subsidies. In general, the most important source is advertising. However, there are considerable differences among various types of media. For many daily newspapers and news weeklies, the share of income that comes from advertising has been estimated at between 50 and 60 percent. For many illustrated magazines, it is 70–80 percent. In American broadcasting, it has been as high as 90–100 percent.[45]

Media owners' appetite for increasing market shares, attracting advertisers, and thereby maximizing profits may get higher priority than journalists' desire to improve the quality and usefulness of medical news reports. Since higher quality often consumes more resources, short-term economic pressures may conflict with the maintenance of high journalistic standards.

To one extent or another, journalists and editors accept economic pressure as a reason to find entertaining stories, even if that means neglecting others that are more significant but decidedly less colorful. This acceptance dates back to the "penny press" that emerged in the 1830s, the forerunner of newspapers as we know them today. Newspapers gradually went from being small-circulation, subscription-based businesses to being mass-circulation, advertising-based businesses. In the 1960s, Walter Sullivan, then science editor of the *New York Times*, defended the responsible light-touch story on economic grounds: "But most newspapers, even perhaps my own, would soon go out of business if they only ran stories of world-shaping significance. We must entertain as well as inform, and it's great fun doing so. Of course, the stories that we print should not be frivolous or in bad taste. . . . What a good newspaper should serve is a balanced diet with plenty of meat and a bit of light, skillfully done pastry."[92]

Awash in a rising tide of other sorts of media outlets, newspapers have to struggle harder all the time to maintain their readership. Critics point out that not only newspapers but also many other outlets are shifting their menu from fine meat and skillfully done pastry to junk food and jello, which cost less to produce, so they can spend more on advertising themselves. The balance between journalists' mission to serve the public with true and significant stories and the media moguls' aim to maximize their companies' profits is becoming increasingly precarious.

Three decades after Walter Sullivan's elegant defense, Anders Rhodiner, deputy editor-in-chief of TT, Sweden's top news agency, crudely summed up his view of the bottom-line realities of selling news and competing with the country's number two news agency:

> News is what my customers pay me for. Our clients need news that sells their papers or keeps their listeners or viewers tuned to their wavelength. Therefore, quality is not the only criterion if a good story on medical news will be published. . . . We are salesmen in a news market which expects stories on talk-of-the-town matters. It is the market that sets the agenda. When all media are reporting on the latest diets, we naturally have to offer our clients a story which fits. If we don't deliver, they will simply turn to another news agency.

Complaining that medical reporters are much too serious, Rhodiner said he wanted more medical stories that could make the audience smile. "I want us to flirt with the market. I am more interested in stories that my clients think their readers want to read than in stories that will get the reporter respectful nods from the scientific community."[80]

Competition for advertising money is also fierce. Medical reporter Andrew Skolnick says that media companies' fear of losing advertisers can interfere with good health reporting.[67] He mentions cigarette advertisers[93–94] as a case in point: "Many women's health magazines in the United States would never do a story about smoking and lung cancer. They are heavily funded by tobacco advertisements. When lung cancer surpassed breast cancer as the number one cancer killer of women in the United States, many did not tell that story. Any other story but not that one."[67] Rebecca Perl of National Public Radio believes some television stations in America are particularly careful not to offend their advertisers by critical reporting: "The people who own these TV stations are somehow getting the message down to their news directors that 'we don't want to be too hard on this or that industry, because they are our advertisers' or 'they own the station.'"[68]

Moreover, competition among stories within a particular news organization may favor quick and simple event-reporting and work against more investigative approaches. The quest for exciting events to fill a daily news quota often outweighs the need for well-researched, critical, in-depth, investigative medical journalism.

Table 2.2.   Shared interests

Journalists	Medical scientists
News	Innovative ideas
Surprise	Unexpected results
Drama	Promising/disappointing results
Impact	Clinically relevant results
Celebrity	Excellence
Personification	Self-promotion

RELIANCE ON SOURCES

Another obstacle to critical, independent medical reporting resembles a *folie à deux* descending on the science writer and the medical expert. In such cases, their interdependence and shared interests (listed in table 2.2) play havoc with both the journalist's duty to be skeptical and the scientist's obligation to question his or her own findings. The media's constant search for news items invites scientists to market new ideas and innovations. Journalists' passion for medical breakthroughs may also coincide with researchers' curiosity about unexpected findings.

Also, the reporter and the expert may share an interest in exaggerating the potential effectiveness of a new treatment or the significance of ongoing resarch.[262] The journalist needs a good story, and the expert needs promotion and visibility to raise the necessary funds. The media's focus on impact and/or usefulness for the general public can be an important concern even for the researcher. They may share enthusiasm for the topic and nourish a hope that the treatment will eventually help patients. For example, when the AIDS epidemic was an emerging topic, network news coverage of potential cures was often misleading, reporting promising treatments but not their subsequent failures.[48] "Promising" scientific findings, when uncritically reported, mix news and views and create false expectations in the audience.

Furthermore, journalists who are inexperienced in medical reporting may believe they are too ignorant to ask relevant questions and to critique expert statements effectively. A similar reluctance to ask provoking questions may arise if a reporter is afraid of spoiling a good relationship with an expert on whom future stories may depend.

The latter situation is probably less common, since most journalists are well aware of this risk. Science writer Deborah Blum notes that she learned early on never to rely on official sources. She adds that "you have to learn quickly that making people angry is a survivable event. Almost everyone gets over it. As long as you get it right, good sources learn to trust you, even when they don't like everything you write."[69] Nevertheless, some reporters' fear of offending a good source—particularly an expert who has a unique position in a small country, state, or region and who is therefore nearly irreplaceable—might keep them from being sufficiently critical.

CONFLICTING INTERESTS

While journalists and scientists sometimes share agendas, their respective focuses of interest may differ markedly (table 2.3). What scientists consider important is not necessarily what journalists are looking for—a difference that may become an impediment to effective reporting. For example, journalists tend to focus on events—preferably sudden events. By contrast, scientific work is often characterized by slow processes, putting together jigsaw puzzles using fragments of knowledge from previous work.

While journalists like to feature individual cases—victims and witnesses—to attract attention and make a story more concrete, scientists like to talk about what the aggregated data show. Many journalists, and others outside the health professions, accept an individual case as sufficient evidence that an intervention is life-saving, useless, or life-threatening. By contrast, medical scientists and epidemiologists often base their analyses on data collected from groups of individuals. For them, an anecdote (a case report) is an insufficient basis for general conclusions about the benefits and risks of an intervention (though it may generate a hypothesis).

While journalists often invite expert sources to speculate, scientists generally aim at verifying or falsifying their hypotheses through systematic observation or experimentation. For example, journalists are usually most interested in a scientific finding's potential utility in patient care. Basic researchers, however, are likely to be more interested in the laboratory results per se than in their clinical applications. Indeed, they may not even have considered whether their results could be used in practice. When journalists encourage them to speculate, their answers can therefore be heavily inflated by enthusiasm, wishful thinking, and self-interest, leading to hyped media reports. Qualifications and details that are important to researchers and crucial to the quality of scientific articles are rarely included in media reports, where the main message is often considered complicated enough.

And while the media tend to polarize views, focusing on conflict, many medical experts strive for consensus. This difference is particularly obvious in tabloid journalism that describes medical discoveries as entirely beneficial or altogether harmful, which creates frustration among experts.[1] To clinicians and scientists, most

Table 2.3. Conflicting focuses of interest

Journalists	Medical scientists
Events	Processes
Individuals (anecdotes)	Groups (aggregated data)
Speculation	Verification/falsification
Clarity	Uncertainty
Simplicity	Qualification
Conflict	Consensus

interventions are a little bit of both. But in the media, experts are expected to take a stand either for or against the procedure in question and to either warn or reassure the audience. Thus, medical news becomes dichotomized.

Avice Meehan, who was previously a reporter and is now vice president of public affairs at Memorial Sloan-Kettering Cancer Center in New York, expands this theme:

> Journalists generally want a lot more from us than we are able to give them in terms of concrete black and white "fabulous-versus-dreadful" messages. Journalists live at the extremes of good and bad, conflict, "cure" or "cause." These things make good stories that sell to their editors and producers. Naturally, reporters want their stories to be on the nightly news, or on page one. But the fact of the matter is that most things they cover are really somewhere in the ambiguous middle.[76]

Although the media are acutely attracted to conflict, they don't always get at the real conflicts.[84] Journalists frequently complain that expert sources are secretive about internal debate. For example, experts may fail to tell reporters about conflicting evidence[95] since doctors and researchers like to project a unified image. Journalists' complaints about medical experts range from failing to alert the press about important news to misleading or actively obstructing reporting.[84,48,96] "They seldom trust us with differences of opinion or conflicting research findings," says Inger Atterstam, an experienced medical reporter at *Svenska Dagbladet*, a major daily newspaper in Sweden.[97]

Dorothy Nelkin also explores the differences between journalistic and scientific agendas.[77] She notes that tensions between the media and scientists arise even though both parties are committed to communicating truth. Their dispute is not necessarily a fight over truth versus falsehood. Instead, it is their views on what is significant and their preferred reporting style that are in conflict. She goes on to suggest that scientists' and journalists' different views of the media's role are perhaps the most important source of conflict. Whereas scientists typically view the media as a conduit or pipeline responsible for transmitting science to the public in a way that can be easily understood, journalists tend to embrace completely different ideals.

PROFESSIONAL IDEALS

Reporters' approach to medical news naturally varies with the type of medium they work for, its format and target groups, and the type of story they are pursuing. In addition, journalists' different professional styles, attitudes, and personal interests may influence their work, resulting in different strengths and weaknesses in reporting.

More specifically, studies of journalists' values have identified three professional styles: the hatchet man, the agitator, and the craftsman.[98-99] These categories are examples of what sociologist Max Weber called "ideal types," categories that accentuate key features of an empirical reality. It is not clear how comprehensive, stable, and universal these categories are. Some reporters may switch style to adapt to a particular assignment. The categories will be used here for didactic purposes.

The hatchet man's top priority is to expose. This reporter approaches those in power with great suspicion. He or she employs unconventional methods to expose the abuse of power and other irregularities among a community's decision makers, ignoring whatever consequences the report may have for individual people or interest groups.[98–99]

The agitator's top priority is to push or lead the audience in a direction that lines up with his or her own basic values and reasons for entering the profession. The selection of facts and interviewees and the slant of the story reflect the agitator's personal biases and views, intentionally or unintentionally. The justification for such an approach is that one can never be completely objective.[98–99]

The craftsman's top priority is to represent facts accurately and to quote a range of sources. He or she would not use unconventional methods or manipulation even when they could lead to uncovering new dimensions in a story. The craftsman is considerate toward interviewees and avoids provoking responses that could put them in an unfavorable light.[98–99]

All three ideal types may have their role in medical reporting. However, all approaches are not equally suitable to a given topic. The journalistic style reporters choose for a particular issue will largely dictate the type of questions asked and will lead them to focus on different aspects of the information that sources provide.

Regardless of what style they employ, reporters need knowledge and experience to do a good job. A key issue is whether the balance among the different styles of reporting is adequate. As we shall see in the next chapter, there may be a tendency among naive medical journalists to not question scientific sources effectively. By contrast, many experienced medical reporters have gained sufficient knowledge about the topic to choose an effective approach, to ask the most important questions, and to change approaches in midstream should the story unfold in an unexpected way.

CHAPTER 3

Scientific Fact or Science Fiction?

Formerly, when religion was strong and science weak, men mistook magic for medicine; now, when science is strong and religion weak, men mistake medicine for magic.
—Thomas Szasz (1920–)

To treat your facts with imagination is one thing, to imagine your facts is another.
—John Burroughs (1837–1921)

Chapter objectives
- **Give examples of stakeholders in the medical media arena**
- **Discuss the concept of truth in the context of medical reporting**
- **Introduce readers to pitfalls in scientific papers**
- **Describe the types of evidence journalists should ask for**

News reporters are generally committed to communicating accurately. They want to inform, comment, scrutinize, and stimulate public debate—even titillate and entertain. Most feel it is their job to know, or find out, if a source is providing heavily biased or misleading information. In a complex field like medicine, this is a great challenge.

If a new treatment is labeled "promising" in the media but in fact has proven ineffective, the story will create false expectations. On the other hand, if reporters fail to alert their audience to the existence of a truly effective treatment, patients may not get access to it quickly enough. If reporters do not inform the public about an actual health hazard, people will take no measures to avoid it, and continued exposure may cause unnecessary harm. Conversely, if reporters signal "danger" when no risk is involved, the public will be unnecessarily alarmed—and perhaps less inclined to trust the media the next time they cry wolf.

The stakeholders are many, and the stakes are high. Since medical media reports can affect decisions at all levels—patients, providers, policymakers, industry—it is crucial that the information supplied is accurate. However, medical news sources may tell less than the whole truth or slant their presentations. Some of their fallacies are related to invalid research results, others to faulty interpretations of solid research.

The trick is for journalists to be aware of these pitfalls so that they can recognize misleading statements and question them. Some critics complain that reporters are careless about how they present medical research,[100–2] but others point out that minor changes in journalistic practice can lead to marked improvements in newspaper articles dealing with medical science.[71,103]

A STORY OF HOPE AND HYPE

The challenges of medical journalism are tremendous. A case in point is a story published by one of the world's leading newspapers: the *New York Times*. On Sunday, May 3, 1998, a science journalist's optimistic report about an alleged cancer cure[104] sparked a media fever across the entire nation. The newsweekly *Time* was fairly derisive in its subsequent cover story:

> Triggered by a front-page medical news story in the usually reserved *New York Times*, all anybody was talking about—on the radio, on television, on the Internet, in phone calls to friends and relatives—was the report that a combination of two new drugs could, as the *Times* put it, "cure cancer in two years." In a matter of hours patients had jammed their doctors' phone lines begging for a chance to test the miracle cancer cure. Investors scrambled to buy a piece of the action, turning the shares of a little company called EntreMed into the most volatile stock on Wall Street. Cancer scientists raced to the phones and fax lines to make sure everyone knew about their research too, generating a new round of headlines and perpetuating the second medical media frenzy in as many weeks. It was Viagra all over again, without the jokes.[105]

The problem was that the new treatment had only been tested on mice, not on humans. The journalist's report was hyped out of all proportion. Acknowledging that there was nothing factually inaccurate about the *New York Times* article, apart from certain omissions, *Time* went on to say that

> this is a case of science journalism gone awry. Although the original article was sprinkled with the necessary caveats, it distorted the significance of EntreMed's research in several important respects, and it exaggerated and romanticized the role of the drug's discoverer, Dr. Judah Folkman, a researcher at Children's Hospital in Boston, in a way that surprised his colleagues and embarrassed Folkman.

The slant of the article and the prominent placement its editors gave it were the key problems, according to *Time*. In addition to interviewing the careful researcher, the journalist had collected quotes of awe and admiration from other experts, including one attributed to James Watson, codiscoverer of DNA's double helix, who was supposed to have said: "Judah is going to cure cancer in two years."

What is particularly interesting about this example is that it comes from an internationally highly respected newspaper with a reputation for being conservative in its news judgment, it was written by an experienced science journalist, and it contains no major inaccuracies. Nevertheless, the article ignited an off-the-scale nationwide reaction to the findings of mouse experiments. This example highlights several subjects explored in this book: the stakeholders in the media arena, the pitfalls of medical science, and what media workers can do to avoid at least the most flagrant mistakes in medical journalism. It points out the science reporter's responsibility to clearly separate scientific facts from science fiction. Dr. Atul Gawande trenchantly remarked about the incident's aftermath in the *New Yorker:* "Reporters quickly move on to write up the next big drug, and doctors are left to react and to improvise, practicing medicine by their wits. It's up to them and to their patients to develop immunity to the recurring epidemics of hype. Journalism, alas, cannot be tested on mice."[106]

THE STAKEHOLDERS, AND THE STRINGS ATTACHED

Traditionally, medical experts have been portrayed by the media as neutral sources of authority. Even incidents of scientific fraud and similar irregularities have often been reported in a manner that idealizes science as a pure and dispassionate profession. This image is unrealistic. By contrast, medical sociologists have compared the media to an arena, where a number of players act, including researchers and clinicians, health authorities, government officials, politicians, health administrators, health insurance organizations, industry representatives, patients, families, and various special-interest organizations. Examples of potential stakeholders are listed in table 3.1.

All of these stakeholders realize that publicity can influence their situation for better or worse, for example, by changing the allocation of resources, public demand, or the policy debate. Self-interest is likely to warp the information that stakeholders provide to the media[34] and may lead to the suppression of facts. For example, medical-

I realize it's a two-for-one deal, but I really don't think my husband wants a mammogram.

Table 3.1. Examples of actors in the medical media arena

Health policymakers
>   Politicians, government officials
>   Administrators of health care, research, education
>   Insurers, payers for health care
>   Labor market representatives (unions, employer organizations)

Health care providers, industry
>   Health professionals
>   Professional societies/associations
>   Hospitals, clinics
>   Pharmaceutical industry
>   Medical-device industry

Health care consumers
>   Patients, families
>   Consumer organizations
>   General public

Scientists, educators, and research councils
>   Research funding authorities/organizations
>   University deans, departments, professors
>   Researchers

Health information brokers
>   Advertising/public-relations agencies
>   Public-information officials
>   Librarians

industry representatives have major economic interests to protect. Researchers who want to promote their own work to improve their reputation[1] and/or secure future funding[101] may avoid questioning their own results. Their claims can be highly colored by concerns for their own careers and their reputations among peers.[16] Politicians may be unduly influenced by political alliances, and bureaucrats by their career concerns and a narrow focus on internal politics. Competition among agencies, sections, and departments may lead bureaucrats to tell half-truths or outright lies. Editors may be pressured by their firms' advertisers or marketing departments or owners.

The need for a critical approach by the media is therefore imperative. When using stakeholders as sources, the critical journalist investigates how they know what they say they know. How representative are their points of view? What are their motives for providing the information? What do they have to gain or lose? Can their statements be verified or at least supported? Can the information they provide be interpreted differently or even be challenged outright by other credible sources? Who else knows? Can the information they provide be confirmed through further investigating and by interviewing other sources? Which of their underlying assumptions should be questioned?

WHAT *IS* TRUTH ANYWAY?

We all have our own truths. Every source, every researcher, every journalist, and every reader/viewer holds a personal view of the world. Some say that one view is as valid as the next. So why is it worthwhile for journalists (or scientists) to search for truth?

Some argue that it is impossible to reflect objective reality—we do not know if such a reality exists. Searching for an objective truth (*objectivism*) is vain. Instead, they argue, journalists should turn to another kind of reporting, where they convey a sense of closeness by expressing personal experiences and emotions (*relativism*). However, it has been suggested that the choice between such untenable extremes is fictitious. Neither of these alternatives is acceptable in journalistic practice.[14]

A different, and perhaps more useful, view of human knowledge is called *critical realism*.[107-8] Those who embrace this concept argue that no description of, or statement about, reality is true in an absolute sense. All knowledge, including news stories, is provisional and more or less fallible. The same reality is understood and described in different ways depending on our social, conceptual, and rhetorical starting points.

However, this does not imply that all knowledge is equally fallible. Neither are all news stories. The validity of statements can be assessed in relation to more or less consensual (intersubjective) experiences of reality.[107-8] Moreover, some scientific studies are better than others as a basis for drawing general conclusions about, for example, the effectiveness of health care procedures.[109-10]

Rhetoric about truth dates back at least to the time of Plato and Aristotle, and the discussion will probably continue as long as philosophers walk the earth. The scope of the debate on truth is potentially limitless. However, for the purposes of medical journalism, this book focuses on the usefulness of analyzing the gap between the best available scientific evidence and the claims made by those who provide a health procedure. If a wide discrepancy exists between promises made to consumers and effects observed in rigorous scientific studies, there is good reason to report this gap. Consumers have a right to expect a health care system that offers them interventions that do more good than harm and that chooses the best available approach. The supporting evidence for a treatment should be generated by generally accepted scientific methods. If not, consumers have a right to know. They also have a right to know about deficiencies in scientific evidence concerning a treatment, and whether they have good reason to question its net benefits.

Faced with an enthusiastic claim—for example, that a new treatment is better than the established ones—some journalists will simply quote the enthusiastic innovator, throwing in a few critical quotes from an expert who thinks that the old methods are better. This approach is convenient and fulfills the superficial requirements of "balanced reporting," but it tends to pit one person's word against another's, a "he-said–she-said" kind of reporting that is not particularly useful. It does not offer the audience much more than could be said in a press release or two. Yet, quoting two parties' opposing comments on an issue is often regarded as "objective" reporting.[14]

So, though it is easier to quote viewpoints than to sort out the truth, this book argues that the "he-said–she-said" approach is insufficient in the context of medical science reporting. True, the audience will learn that two experts disagree (which is almost always the case). This might in itself be interesting. But the audience is left without knowing whether any solid evidence actually supports either of the claims. The increased value that skilled medical reporters can add comes from the critical scrutiny of expert judgments. Critical reporters will question to what extent expert sources can support their statements, giving their audience at least a hint of the substance behind the words.

A drastic example: If a journalist were to simply report that one doctor says crystals can cure cancer and that another doctor claims that this is nonsense, the report would not provide any useful information. Shrugging shoulders, the reporter could say, "Who am I to know what the experts don't?" A far better approach would be to ask: "What basis do they have for these claims? Are there decent studies to verify or disprove them? Who seems to be closer to the truth?" Andrew Skolnick, investigative medical reporter, says: "Our job is to tell the truth, not to balance truth with lies. Lies are not equal to truth, and should not be given the same weight. We [journalists] are supposed to weigh the information, not to balance it."[67]

Journalists can often find reasons to dig deeper into the scientific basis of seemingly authoritative expert statements. Considering the potential biases of experts and other stakeholders, and the flaws of medical science, medical journalists need at least a basic understanding of scientific methods and of problems associated with claims of benefits and risks. A basic familiarity with pitfalls in science will allow reporters to ask critical questions. In some cases, it is impossible to judge who can best substantiate his or her claims. That, too, is an important piece of information.

Medical researchers use both experimental and nonexperimental (observational) studies. The two differ considerably. In an experimental study, the researcher manipulates a variable—for instance, a certain risk factor—to see if it affects morbidity. In a nonexperimental study, the investigator observes a real-life situation as it is and draws conclusions from those observations. Both experimental and observational approaches are useful and indeed complementary. They also have different strengths and weaknesses.

Experimental studies generally allow more control over factors other than the one being studied. Fewer factors can interfere with the targeted issue. On the other hand, experimental settings can become so controlled and artificial that their results no longer apply to real-life situations. This is particularly true for many laboratory studies.

Observational studies have the inverse problem. Since they deal with real-life situations and make no attempt to manipulate reality, extraneous factors can affect the results, leading to false conclusions. These factors are commonly known as *confounders,* factors that distort the true relationship of the study variables. Confounders are related to the outcome of interest but are extraneous to the study question and unequally distributed among the groups being compared.

For example, in a study of infant leukemia that compares infants living near high-voltage cables to others who do not, exposure to car exhaust fumes is a potential confounder. Children who live near high-voltage cables (which are frequently located near freeways) may *also* be more exposed to exhaust fumes, which may contribute to the risk for disease. In this case, any possible harmful effect of high-voltage cables may be overestimated. It is impossible to keep track of all potential confounders.

SCIENTIFIC EVALUATION OF THE BENEFITS OF HEALTH CARE

Many scientific studies—experimental and observational—do not meet even the most basic quality criteria. Medical reporters have good reason to be skeptical of research results, even those published in peer-reviewed journals. As Dr. David Sackett, a leading proponent for evidence-based medicine, puts it: "There are only a handful of ways to do a study properly but a thousand ways to do it wrong." Many published studies should not be used as a basis for health care decisions.[110] If their results were implemented, they might do more harm than good.

Dr. Margaret Winker, deputy editor of the *Journal of the American Medical Association* (*JAMA*), reviews manuscripts submitted to the journal. "We reject almost half of all manuscripts even before formal peer review," she says.[111] Reasons vary, but Dr. Winker thinks it is obvious that health professionals need to know more about research methodology and epidemiology. Common quality problems include underpowered studies too small to answer the questions posed, case series in which authors draw conclusions even though no hypothesis has been tested, and case control studies in which cases and controls have been recruited from different populations. Furthermore, cohort studies with many dropouts and surveys with a response rate below 60 percent are unlikely to be accepted by *JAMA*, according to Dr. Winker.

Other reasons for misleading results include study designs that do not use control groups or are otherwise inappropriate, studies that have significant conflicts of interest, and studies that employ incorrect or inappropriate statistical analyses.[112]

Even when studies are properly executed, they can still have fatal problems. "Data dredging is quite common," says Dr. Winker. "It means that the authors go on a 'fishing expedition,' that is, perform so many comparisons and analyses of subsets of their data that some associations are bound to be statistically significant just by chance."[111] Instead of accepting that their initial hypothesis was not confirmed, the investigators keep looking for statistically significant associations until they find one. If they just keep analyzing the data, they are bound to find some association produced by chance alone.* If other researchers repeat the study, they probably will not find that association.

---

*The statistical reason is the following: Associations with a 5 percent or lower probability of being produced by chance alone are commonly accepted as "statistically significant." This means that, on average, for every twenty analyses performed, one will show an association even when there is none. This association will be a "false positive." Such is the play of chance. Data dredging is similar to throwing dice—if you keep throwing them long enough, chance alone will produce 5 sixes or 8 threes in a row or some other seemingly noteworthy result.

Table 3.2. General questions related to scientific quality in clinical trials

- Did the researchers decide on a hypothesis (or a clear question) before designing the study?
- Was the study designed in a way that makes it possible to confirm or reject that hypothesis (or answer that question)?
- Does the experiment group represent the population concerned, and is the sample size sufficient?
- Is there an acceptable comparison group?
- Are measurements and assessments of outcomes reliable?
- Is all relevant information reported?
- Have all undesired or irrelevant factors (confounders) that could influence the results been considered?
- Are the results analyzed using the appropriate statistical methods?

Some general questions a critical reader should ask to determine the scientific quality of clinical trials are listed in table 3.2. As one becomes more acquainted with scientific reports, one will come to recognize some hallmarks and warning flags quite easily. The following topics (adapted from Greenhalgh)[113] give a basic understanding of some pitfalls in scientific papers.

1. How was the hypothesis framed?

A clear and specific hypothesis, framed before the study is designed, is one of many clues to carefully planned, good research. A hypothesis is a statement that says, for example, "Drug A lowers serum LDL cholesterol more than a placebo in Caucasian men aged forty to sixty years who have a raised serum cholesterol level, with LDL cholesterol over 160 mg/dL." Note that the outcome measured here is serum low-density lipoprotein (LDL) cholesterol alone—not cardiovascular disease or premature death. Hence, conclusions can be drawn only for serum LDL cholesterol levels. Drug A's effects on disease or premature death must be *measured* if such conclusions are to be drawn.

The hypothesis should be as specific as possible, including, for example, a connection between two or more factors (*variables*) or a difference between two groups (such as an experimental group and a control group). In this example, the control group would receive a placebo (a dummy or "inactive" treatment), the hypothesis being that serum cholesterol in the group receiving drug A will be lower. (The two groups should be treated similarly in all other respects—for example, both groups should receive identical dietary advice.)

A clear hypothesis makes a good start. Conversely, a fuzzy hypothesis, framed after the data were collected, can be a clue to a poor study. The study may have been a fishing expedition where so many questions were asked that chance alone would produce one or two statistically significant results. (Qualitative studies, even good ones, frequently do not use hypotheses as starting points. Instead, as discussed below, they formulate questions and explore issues in a more open-ended fashion, a process by which hypotheses may be generated.)

At times, hypotheses are phrased in the negative, stating that there is no connection between the variables under study or no difference between the treatment groups compared. Such statements are known as *null hypotheses*. Investigators using null hypotheses typically aim at disproving them—they attempt to *rule out* the possibility that the groups under study are similar or that no connection exists.

2. What methods were chosen to test the hypothesis?

Many problems occur because investigators often fail to use the best possible method to test their hypotheses. The critical journalist starts by asking whether the threshold has been met. Did the investigator describe the study design and method in detail? Did the sample of subjects match the hypothesis? Were there enough subjects to detect differences of the expected magnitude? (Researchers should calculate the appropriate sample size when the study is designed and report what method they chose for that purpose.)

The sample of subjects must match the category of patients in which the results would be applied. Studies should clearly describe how participants were recruited (e.g., by advertisements, written invitations to patients at one specific clinic), what selection criteria were used, the age and sex distribution of the group, and any other relevant characteristics of the participants. If participants are not representative of the larger group of patients in all important respects, results are likely to be misleading. The conclusions will probably be false.

If a control group exists (one should, if the effectiveness of a treatment is studied), remember that the same attention must be paid to the control group as to the experimental group (sometimes called the intervention group or the treatment group). Both groups (not just the experimental group) must be relevant and representative, and all measuring must be done in the same way in both groups. If, for example, investigators are interested in the effect of a cholesterol-lowering drug on the risk for myocardial infarction and premature death, and there are more heavy tobacco smokers in the control group than in the treatment group, the beneficial effect of the drug will probably be overestimated. Ideally, the control group is identical to the experimental group in all respects except the treatment they receive.

3. How was the test carried out?

A good study design can be spoiled if researchers fail to follow the protocol carefully. For example, random numbers, either from tables or generated by computer, should be used to assign subjects to experimental or control groups. The conditions under which the readings are taken should be standardized to the extent possible.

Response rates are key to the validity of a study's results. A small sample with a good response rate is often preferable to a large sample with a poor response rate. Once a person is in a study sample, researchers must pursue him or her with relentless determination to obtain an observation/response. Any substitution violates the randomness of the sample and threatens the validity of the study's results.[114]

At times, researchers are unable to follow their original plans for practical reasons. If this happens, it must be made clear in the final report. For example, patients may drop out of the study altogether, fail to follow the treatment plan, be forced to switch to some other treatment, or fail to present themselves for follow-up. Investigators should be able to foresee most of these problems in pilot studies. All deviations from the protocol must be noted and considered when interpreting the results.

4. How were the data analyzed and reported?

Simple analyses, for example, statistical *means* and *medians,* should be reported before the results of advanced statistics are reported. Some measure of variation around these numbers must also be included, showing how the results are distributed.

When researchers choose a statistical method, they need to make certain assumptions about the material. For example, they often assume that measurements are distributed according to a symmetrical, bell-shaped curve. If these assumptions are wrong, the investigators will choose an inappropriate method of analysis, and the results are likely to be false. Sometimes, only a statistician can tell if the right method has been used. Readers of scientific studies should be on their guard if the researchers have used unusual or very sophisticated methods.

The play of chance is always present. The fewer the subjects or the lower the number of observations, the greater the influence of chance. The probability that the results can be attributed to chance, that is, *statistical significance,* must always be reported. It is expressed by a *p-value* or a *confidence interval.*

Sometimes, subgroups of data are analyzed separately. The use of many *subgroup analyses* should alert journalists to be suspicious, since the risk is great that a statistically significant result has been produced by chance. Researchers should not draw too heavily on subgroup results.

If confounders were present, these should be described along with the attempts to compensate for them in the analysis. Subjects crossing over between experimental and control groups must be noted. They should be included in their original group when analyzing the results.

5. How was the analysis interpreted?

Possible bias and alternative explanations should be considered. Are the conclusions based firmly on the results of the study, and are they reasonable with respect to previous findings? Even if results are statistically significant, authors sometimes draw conclusions that are not supported by their results. Dr. Margaret Winker of *JAMA* comments:

> We see quite often that the results are valid, but the authors take their conclusions too far. . . . Even well-performed studies often come with interpretations that are completely distorted and do not reflect the results. In this context, it makes me nervous to know that some pharmaceutical companies let their marketing departments look at all papers before they are published. We have seen, for example, clinically irrelevant findings get overemphasized, while toxicity information is played down.[111]

One should therefore check whether all results are considered in the conclusions, or only the ones that support the hypothesis. Side effects should always be included, as should results that point in a different direction. If conclusions are new and surprising, check whether they apply to the whole study and are consistent for all subjects and subgroups.

Where authors conclude that an association exists between two variables, this is more likely to be true if there is also a dose-response relationship (e.g., the higher the dose, the greater the effect).

Negative results (i.e., the absence of statistically significant differences or associations) are deceptive and must be interpreted with caution. The fact that no difference or association was found does not mean it does not exist. The simple reason is often that the study is too small to detect a modest difference or a weak association. Very large studies are needed to conclude that a difference or relation probably does not exist.

Also remember that a single study is rarely powerful enough to draw safe conclusions. New results should be interpreted in the context of previous findings.

Another key issue is whether conclusions apply to all patients, or whether they cannot be generalized due to the selection of a narrow range of subjects.

EVIDENCE USED IN VERIFYING OR DISPROVING MEDICAL CLAIMS

When questioning the accuracy of medical claims, it is useful to consult the best available scientific evidence. Usually, the best sources of evidence on the effectiveness of a *treatment* are well-performed meta-analyses of the results from randomized controlled trials.[115] For *risk factors*, cohort studies typically offer the best evidence, while the best sources for *diagnostic tests* are blinded comparisons of the test with a standard.[116]

One of the most common claims is that a new treatment is superior to existing alternatives. Some types of studies are generally more reliable than others when it comes to showing the efficacy of different treatments. The following sections rank the types of studies from the most to the least reliable in making general recommendations based on efficacy.[109,117]

Table 3.3. Critical differences between systematic and narrative reviews (reprinted with permission)[118]

Feature	Narrative (conventional) review	Systematic review
Question	Often broad in scope	Often focused on a clinical question
Sources and search	Usually not specified, potentially biased search strategy	Comprehensive search of sources and explicit search strategy
Selection	Usually not specified, potentially biased coverage	Criterion-based selection, uniformly applied
Appraisal	Variable	Rigorous critical appraisal
Synthesis	Often a qualitative summary	Quantitative summary
Inferences	Sometimes evidence-based	Usually evidence-based

1. Systematic reviews and meta-analyses

A systematic review is a review of all the individual studies that focus on a particular research question, including their methods and results. This is a relatively new type of review article that has evolved alongside the evidence-based medicine movement. Like conventional review articles, systematic reviews summarize and synthesize original studies, but they are different in important respects. Systematic reviews are supposed to be comprehensive and should use explicit, reproducible criteria in the selection and exclusion of articles for review. Studies are identified and selected, and their results are assessed, in a systematic fashion. The results of the individual studies (commonly randomized controlled trials) may be pooled in a meta-analysis. Meta-analyses use statistical techniques to integrate the quantitative results of the studies included. This increases the sample size, with the aim of making the overall result more reliable than the result of each individual study. Table 3.3 summarizes the critical differences between systematic and narrative reviews.

2. Randomized controlled trials

A classic randomized controlled trial is an experiment in which participants are randomly assigned to an intervention group or a comparison group. Two key criteria need to be met. The first is *randomization;* that is, participants are allocated by a random, unbiased method (equivalent to flipping a coin). The second criterion is that a *control group* must be used; for instance, the persons receiving one type of treatment are compared with others who receive a placebo or a specific, different treatment.

The term *random* does not mean "haphazard" but has a precise technical meaning. Randomization means that each subject has an equal chance of being given each treatment, but nobody can predict which will be given to whom. In practice, no coins are flipped. Most investigators use either a table of random numbers or a random-number generator in a computer to perform randomized allocation.[119] Alternating between treatments is not the same as randomization.

The randomization process is used to even out differences between the groups that might otherwise interfere with the results. The purpose is to balance out both measurable and unmeasurable factors, ensuring a fair comparison. The process also prevents a researcher from consciously or subconsciously allocating subjects in a biased way.

Ideally, randomized controlled trials are also *double blind;* that is, both researchers and subjects are kept ignorant of who is receiving which treatment. Allocation is not disclosed until the study is completed and the statistical analysis has been performed.

3. Nonrandomized controlled trials

Experimental trials that use a control group for comparison but do not allocate subjects to experimental or control groups by a random method are likely to yield results that are more or less distorted by different methodologial biases.[120] There is a significant risk of imbalance between the groups. The imbalance may or may not be obvious, which can produce misleading results.

The reason for at least having a control group is that trial subjects' health may improve for reasons other than the intervention. For example, it has been shown that many health problems improve spontaneously over time. A treatment study should be able to demonstrate improvement *over and above* any background improvement shown by a control group. The control group should receive some other treatment or a placebo rather than nothing at all. Otherwise, a different outcome in the intervention group can be due to some nonspecific effect of getting more attention than the control group does or to mere expectations that they will get better because they are being treated.

If an expert makes statements on the basis of a nonrandomized controlled clinical trial, critical reporters question whether the intervention and control groups were really equal in all important respects except the treatment. There is no way the expert can guarantee this, since many important factors are either still unknown or difficult to measure. Researchers can only attempt to make statistical adjustments for all known important differences. Again, the best way to prevent bias is to randomize.

4. Cohort studies

A cohort study is nonexperimental. It observes the relationship between an exposure, or risk factor, and one or more outcomes. A group of persons (a cohort) who share some common characteristic, for instance, exposure to a suspected health risk, are followed over a period of time and are compared with a nonexposed cohort. The follow-up period is usually long—years or even decades—since many diseases develop slowly, particularly some cancers. The cohort's level of exposure is established at the beginning of the study. Two common sources of bias are people dropping out of the study and observer bias in follow-up of exposed and nonexposed groups.

5. Case control studies

Case control studies are nonexperimental. Like cohort studies, they typically investigate the relationship between exposure to a suspected health risk and developing a disease. However, unlike cohort studies, the individuals are not followed to see if they become ill. Instead, patients who are known to have a particular disease are identified and compared with a group of people who do not have that disease. Both groups' past exposure to a suspected risk factor is then traced through medical records or by asking them to recall such exposure. The process of selecting the comparison group is called "matching," since the subjects in the comparison group are carefully selected to be as similar as possible to those who are ill. A perfect match is of course not possible. However, this study design is usually the only option for investigating rare diseases.

6. Cross-sectional studies

This is yet another type of nonexperimental study. Through interviews and/or tests, it describes a representative sample of persons from a particular category. All data are collected on a single occasion (instead of over a long period of time). The sample must be randomly selected from the larger population under study because this is the only way to avoid results being influenced by the particular characteristics of volunteers. A typical question asked in this type of study is: How common is this disease in this particular group?

7. Case reports

The medical histories of individual patients are called case reports or anecdotes. Sometimes, several cases are recorded in the same fashion, to form a case series. Case series are commonly used to track rare side effects or to lay the groundwork for a larger study.

All research methods have their particular strengths and weaknesses. They do not exclude each other but should be used in different situations to answer different questions (see table 3.4). Although they top the list above, randomized controlled trials cannot answer all important clinical questions. For example, rare side effects need to be detected by case reports. Moreover, for a particular research question, even weaker studies may generate hypotheses that can be tested using stronger designs.

However, it is important to remember the general rule that case series, cross-sectional surveys, or case control studies cannot give valid, reliable answers to questions such as, is this treatment generally better than another one?

Nonrandomized study designs can detect associations between an intervention and an outcome. But they cannot rule out the possibility that the association was caused by a third factor linked to both intervention and outcome. If an expert claims that a certain treatment is generally superior for a certain condition, the sources of evidence needed to evaluate that claim are randomized controlled trials or meta-analyses of such trials.

A few rules of thumb can be useful for journalists who wish to question the evidence for general recommendations about treatments:[117]

- Prospective studies are preferable to retrospective studies.
- Controlled studies are preferable to uncontrolled studies.
- Randomized studies are preferable to nonrandomized ones.
- Large studies (i.e., those including many subjects) are preferable to small ones.
- Contemporaneous controls (control groups investigated at the same time as those not acting as controls) are preferable to historical controls.
- Blinded studies are preferable to unblinded studies.

THE BEST INTENTIONS, BUT . . .

Once one knows what type of evidence to look for, the second issue is whether or not the study was rigorously performed. Any type of study can be unreliable if it has not been carried out carefully. For example, results from a poorly designed and executed randomized controlled trial may be less reliable than the results of a rigorous but nonrandomized controlled study. A rank ordering of methods thus assumes that each is properly designed and executed. A well-designed and well-executed study that is lower on the list may give more accurate results than a poorly designed and poorly executed study that is higher on the list.

TRIAL BASICS: BIG ENOUGH, LONG ENOUGH, TIGHT ENOUGH?

In statistics, size lends power—the power to find an effect if it is actually there. As the number of cases increases, so does the probable accuracy of a conclusion. Conversely, the smaller the number of observations, the less likely it is that the conclusion is valid.

Thus, a critical issue in most studies aiming to make generalizations about treatment/exposure effects is: Was the sample big enough? The general rule is that a trial

Table 3.4. Evidence to look for and some related critical issues

Treatment (e.g., drugs, surgery)—meta-analyses, randomized trials
Critical issues:
1. Was the assignment of patients to treatments completely randomized (or could there be systematic differences between intervention and control groups at the onset of the study)?
2. Were all patients who entered the study accounted for at its conclusion (or was there a systematic difference between the groups with respect to dropouts or withdrawals)?
3. Were all patients, health professionals, and research leaders "blind" to the treatment (or were only the patients unaware of which treatment they received)?
4. Were the intervention group and the control group cared for in exactly the same way, apart from the treatment under study (or were there other systematic differences)?
5. Were all relevant outcomes measured (or only the ones that interested the researchers)?
6. Were the outcomes assessed in exactly the same way in both groups (or was the control group measured differently)?
7. Was follow-up sufficiently long and complete (or was the study ended before all relevant outcomes, including long-term effects, could be observed)?
8. Are the patients in the study similar to real-life patients (or were they so narrowly selected that they represent a small minority)?

Risk factors—cohort studies (if common disease) or case control studies (if rare disease); case reports may also provide crucial information
Critical issues:
1. Were the groups similar with respect to important determinants of outcome, other than the one of interest (or were their prospects different)?
2. Was there adjustment for differences between the groups in important prognostic factors (or were these differences ignored or simply noted)?
3. Were exposures and outcomes measured in the same way in the groups being compared (or was the control group measured differently)?
4. In cohort studies: Was follow-up sufficiently long and complete (or was it terminated before all relevant outcomes, including long-term effects, could be observed)?

Diagnostic tests—cross-sectional surveys, where the test is compared with a gold standard (i.e., a reference method that is known to consistently give the correct diagnosis)
Critical issues:
1. Has the diagnostic test been evaluated in a patient sample that included both mild and severe, treated and untreated disease, plus individuals with disorders that might masquerade as the disease being studied (i.e., has the diagnostic test been evaluated in an appropriate spectrum of patients on whom it will be used in clinical practice)?

(continued)

Table 3.4. Evidence to look for and some related critical issues *(continued)*

2. Was the new method compared independently and blindly against a gold standard? Typically, gold standard tests are invasive and/or expensive diagnostic methods, but they can be used in studies to validate the performance of simpler/cheaper methods. However, gold standards are rarely 100 percent accurate. They are simply the best method of diagnosis according to current dogma.[121]
3. Are the intervention group and the control group really equal in age, gender mix, socioeconomic status, smoking/drinking habits, presence of coexisting illness, etc. (or are there differences, apart from the risk exposure, that might contribute to the outcome)?
4. Is the target disease dangerous if left undiagnosed (or is it relatively harmless)?
5. Is there an effective treatment for the disease, or are there other benefits of a diagnosis (or does the test simply lead to awareness of a condition that will be left untreated anyway)?
6. Has the risk involved in performing the test been studied, and is it acceptable to the patient (or is the test itself harmful, painful, or uncomfortable)?
7. How common are "false alarms" (false-positive test results) and missed diagnoses (false-negative results), and how severe are the consequences?

Screening tests (diagnostic tests that can be used in large populations to discover disease before it causes symptoms)—cross-sectional surveys
Critical issues:
1. Were subjects really randomly sampled from the larger population of interest (or were subjects recruited as volunteers, e.g., through advertising or by asking patients at a particular clinic)?
2. Were the test and reference standards measured independently (blind) of each other?
3. Was the test measured independently of all other clinical information?
4. Has early treatment (after a true-positive test result) been shown to improve prognosis?
5. Is the test relatively simple, not harmful, and acceptable to the patient?
6. How common are false alarms and missed diagnoses, and how severe are the consequences?

should be large enough to have a high chance of detecting, as statistically significant, a worthwhile effect if it exists, and thus to be reasonably certain that no benefit exists if it is not found in the trial.[122]

Small studies are also more vulnerable to random variations and systematic errors, and dramatic findings are often completely misleading. Nevertheless, such studies often make headlines. A ludicrous example is the front-page story "Fat Foods Make You Sharp,"[123] recently published by a tabloid. According to the article, a researcher had studied eight men, asking them to rate their own alertness after having consumed foods rich in either carbohydrates or fats. Although the sample was vanishingly small, no control group was used, and the measurements had been limited to self-reported sleepiness, the journalist reported without qualification the general conclusion that "you can concentrate better and get less tired if you eat fat food." It should not be difficult to be more critical.

A second critical issue in clinical studies is whether the follow-up was long enough. Obviously, longer studies consume more resources, which is one reason many researchers do not follow subjects long enough to be able to draw sound conclusions. Reporters should find out whether the follow-up continued long enough for the effect of the treatment or exposure to be observable and to show whether or not the effects (and side effects) were lasting.

Third, it is important to ask how many participants did not complete the study as planned. Withdrawal and dropout from studies are common problems that may give misleading results. Subjects' reasons for leaving the study must be described in detail, including side effects (actual or suspected), unexpected changes in health status, loss of motivation, or moving to another area. Unless it can be demonstrated that dropout was random in all important respects, the conclusions based on the remaining subjects may be false.

Simply ignoring everyone who has withdrawn from a clinical trial will bias the results, usually in favor of the intervention.[124] Therefore, in their statistical analysis, researchers are supposed to keep all subjects in the group to which they were *originally* assigned, regardless of what happens during the course of the study (intention-to-treat analysis).[125] Everyone assigned to the control group must be analyzed together with that group, even if they had to switch to the intervention group, for example, and actually received the treatment. If some patients who were originally in the control group ended up receiving the treatment and were analyzed with the control group, that would affect the results in the control group. The control group would be "contaminated." Failing to analyze results according to the original intention to treat defeats the purpose of randomization.

CHAPTER 4

Observation, Interpretation, Persuasion

He who wants to persuade should put his trust not in the right argument, but in the right word. The power of sound has always been greater than the power of sense.

Joseph Conrad (1857–1924)

A few observations and much reasoning lead to error; many observations and a little reasoning lead to truth.

Alexis Carrel (1873–1944), surgeon and biologist

Chapter objectives
- **Describe the qualitative approach in health care research**
- **Suggest ways to scrutinize arguments and reasoning**
- **Discuss why "promising" treatments must be questioned**

THE QUALITATIVE APPROACH

Some health care researchers are not interested in questions like "Which of the treatments is most effective in reducing these symptoms?" and do not carry out experiments. Instead, they focus on interpreting phenomena in terms of the meanings people bring to them. Their studies, if carried out properly, explore questions like "What is it like to live with chronic pain?" or "Why do HIV-infected people have unprotected sex?" The investigators choose a *hermeneutic* (interpretive) approach, and their purpose is often to reach a deeper understanding of a phenomenon. Description and interpretation are key concepts.

These are *qualitative* research methods. Investigators using qualitative methods have to tackle as many methodological problems as researchers using quantitative methods, but the main problems are different. Interpretations in qualitative studies can be even more deceptive than measurements used in quantitative research.

Qualitative research methods have been developed within the humanities, in disciplines like history and philosophy, and are sometimes used in such fields as nursing research and organizational studies. In their work, researchers might use interviews, letters, and patient diaries.

Qualitative studies generate ideas and hypotheses through inductive reasoning. Inferences are made through induction, which means reasoning from the particular case to the general. (By contrast, quantitative research uses deductive reasoning, i.e., from the general to the particular.) If researchers observe, for example, that HIV-infected people under study have unprotected sex because they are too embarrassed to use a condom, they might conclude through inductive reasoning that this is a general problem for the HIV-infected population.

Good qualitative research employs a range of approaches for each problem. The validity of qualitative methods is enhanced by using a combination of research methods (a process called triangulation) and by independent analysis of the data by more than one researcher.[126]

Qualitative studies do not need a statistically representative sample of the population under study, since they do not focus on the average. It can be more important to select subjects who are able to describe their experiences, views, and situations.

The critical reporter must always keep in mind that qualitative research and quantitative research cannot answer the same questions. The fields of application are different. It is inappropriate, for example, to use a qualitative study analyzing the diary of a woman with breast cancer to draw conclusions about which cytostatic is the most effective in reducing breast tumors. Conversely, a randomized controlled trial does not give a good understanding of how women treated by chemotherapy cope with fatigue and nausea.

It may be difficult for a medical reporter to determine the scientific value of a qualitative study. Trisha Greenhalgh, senior lecturer at the Department of Primary Care and Population Sciences, University College London Medical School, has suggested a list of important questions that should be asked when evaluating the quality of qualitative studies.[126] Some key issues may be relevant to medical reporters who report on qualitative research, including:

1. Was there a clearly formulated question or set of questions (or was the focus of the study unclear)?
2. Was a qualitative approach appropriate (or would a quantitative study have been better suited to address the research question)?
3. Do the specific aspects of the study design and the methods fit the questions asked?
4. How were the setting and subjects selected? Are they described in sufficient detail?
5. Are the methods used well founded and described in sufficient detail (or is the description simply reduced to a reference to someone else's work)? Were the data analyzed in a systematic way?
6. Were there any attempts to analyze aspects that contradict or challenge the theory at issue (or were such anomalies simply ignored)?
7. Are the results credible and clinically important (or do they make no sense or seem irrelevant)?

8. Are the researchers' conclusions justified by the results (or does their analysis fail to explain why people behaved in a certain way)? Are the conclusions consistent with what is already known?

SCRUTINIZING ARGUMENTS AND REASONING

It is possible to establish whether someone's reasoning is correct or incorrect, regardless of whether or not we agree with the person. According to logic, certain patterns of thinking do lead from truth to truth whereas others do not. Thus, it is useful to analyze how we may be led to believe something.

First, a distinction can be made between two kinds of inference. When experts claim that the truth of their premises *guarantees* the truth of their conclusion, they are using *deductive inference*. Deductive reasoning holds to a very high standard of correctness. The premises must provide absolute and complete support for the conclusion. If the inference is deductive, it would be inconsistent to suppose that the premises are true but the conclusion false.

When experts claim that the truth of their premises merely *makes it likely or probable* that the conclusion is also true, they are using *inductive inference*. Inductive arguments need adequate observations to substantiate claims. However, the standard of correctness for inductive reasoning is much more flexible. Inductive arguments can be stronger or weaker in the sense that their conclusions have a higher or lower probability of being correct.

Induction is often described as moving from the specific case to the general, whereas deduction begins with the general and ends with the specific case. Arguments that are based on observation or experience are better expressed inductively, while arguments based on laws, rules, or other widely accepted principles are better expressed deductively.

Some inductive arguments are comparisons, or analogies, between two phenomena. For example, a physician is making an inductive argument when he or she says, "Every time I have prescribed this medication for high blood pressure, my patients have suffered headaches. Now that I am prescribing the same medication to this patient, he will suffer from a headache." An analogy is made between previous experiences and the present situation. According to logic, the strength of an inductive argument depends largely on three factors:

1. the accuracy and comprehensiveness of the previous observations (Did the physician really prescribe this medication, and did the previous patients really suffer headaches?),
2. the strength of the causal link (Were the headaches really caused by the medication, or did they simply coincide with it?),
3. the similarity of the compared situations (Are there really no significant differences between this patient and the previous patients?).

Let us assume that an expert argues: "All men should have the X test, since it leads to early diagnosis of Y cancer." The expert refers to a study that shows that X detects Y with a high degree of precision and reliability. The following steps can be followed to see if the conclusion is true.

1. Identify the *main thesis*, or main statement. This is generally what the persuader is trying to lead us to believe—the conclusion that he or she has drawn. Is it clear and precise? In this case, the statement "all men should have the X test" is clear, but we may want to find out, for example, if it applies to all age-groups, even men who are nearing their hundredth birthday.
2. Find the *premises*, that is, the statements that form the foundation on which the main thesis builds. Conclusions are frequently based on a number of premises—stated or implied. In our example, the only explicit premise is "X leads to early diagnosis of Y."
3. *Evaluate* the stated premises. First, are they true or false? Is there scientific evidence to verify or refute them? Second, are the premises really relevant to the main thesis, or do they refer to a different situation? To evaluate the premise "X leads to early diagnosis of Y," we may first need to look closely at the study to which the expert refers and find out whether or not the study actually demonstrates just that. Then, we may want to ask whether "Y cancer," when diagnosed by X, includes all forms of the disease.
4. Find potential *unstated premises*. These statements belong to the argument, even though they are only implicit. In our example, they could be "early diagnosis prolongs life" and "prolonging life is good."
5. *Evaluate* all these underlying assumptions, one at a time. Are they true or false, relevant or irrelevant? Is there scientific evidence to verify or refute them? If they reflect value judgments, would people really agree? In the stated example, most people would probably agree that prolonging life is good, at least if your quality of life is acceptable. However, let us assume that we find out that there is no effective treatment against the disease. Even if Y cancer is treated at an early stage, patients' survival is not affected. Then one of the premises—"early diagnosis prolongs life"—would, in fact, be false. Hence, the main thesis should be rejected in the next step.
6. *Accept or reject* the main thesis, after weighing the truth and relevance of its premises.

Note that *reasoning* to show that a claim is true or false, as illustrated above, is different from describing the *history* of a claim. If experts say: "We believe this treatment is effective because we have used it for decades," they are not presenting an argument for the treatment's effectiveness. They are merely giving an account—perhaps a true one—of the historical motive for their belief. The history of medicine is rife with examples of ineffective and even harmful procedures and treatments that nevertheless continued to be used. The effectiveness of these interventions was not questioned. One such procedure is bloodletting, which was widely used to treat all kinds of symptoms.

Another example is radiation therapy against pain in the shoulders, neck, and back, which was considered effective as recently as the 1950s. Later, it was shown that such treatment had no effect and in fact increased the incidence of leukemia. A third example is bed rest following myocardial infarction. Although it sounds reasonable that the heart should rest, research has shown that extended bed rest is harmful.

Arguments that seem convincing at first may have severe flaws when analyzed further. Persuasive wording may conceal weak arguments—a truth that was already acknowledged in ancient Greece. Three classic categories of persuasion—logos, ethos, and pathos—were identified by Aristotle (384–322 B.C.).

Logos, appeal to rationality, will include facts, figures, and expert statements. These will reassure reporters who are unsure of the facts and will tend to dehumanize sensitive issues. An argument may focus in great detail on scientific verification but overlook key ethical issues. Moreover, as discussed elsewhere in this book, opinions, which may be completely without factual support, are often confused with facts. Statistics can be misused. The use of exact numbers can create a false impression of knowledge, precision, and objectivity. Important information may be left out. Decimal points and the like should be used for meaning, not for emphasis.[114]

Ethos, ethical appeal, is used to create an image of credibility, competence, integrity, attractiveness, and power. The source will appear credible and reliable, gaining persuasive power not only by demonstrating knowledge and expertise but also by coming across as a generally trustworthy and reliable person. However, the critical reporter will not allow a source's impressive academic titles, affiliation with well-reputed organizations, high social status, or generally authoritative appearance to derail a critical analysis.

Pathos, appeal to emotion, includes examples and narratives intended to arouse the target. It will humanize issues, engage the audience, and may be so overwhelming as to overshadow rationality. Statements may seem justified because the alleged consequences are so desirable. In these cases, it is easy to forget to ask if the premises are really true. Furthermore, the examples and testimonies used in the emotional appeal might have been taken out of context or may be so outdated or unqualified that they are irrelevant.

Logos, ethos, and pathos are sometimes accompanied by a fourth concept—*mythos,* appeal to culture, which associates proposals with cultural traditions, attitudes, and values. This technique is widely used in advertising to imply that a product is beneficial because of its relation to phenomena that are already widely accepted in a certain culture.

Commonly used persuasive techniques include repetition, analogies, distractions, and generalizations. Repetition of a statement—in different settings, for example, or by different people—will increase its persuasive effect. Analogies or metaphors may lead the audience to a desired conclusion. The analogy is usually a clear-cut case, picked to prove a point. However, such a comparison may not be justified if the phenomena compared are too dissimilar. Distractions, red herrings, may be introduced by sources when they want to draw reporters' attention away from the central issue. By introducing a new, exciting item, the source may be able to avoid discussing a sensitive issue. Finally, erroneous generalizations can be made.

Critical journalists must be constantly aware of different persuasive techniques when interviewing sources, attending press conferences, and scrutinizing news releases.

FOUR REASONS TO QUESTION "PROMISING" TREATMENTS

Four important questions may help reporters maintain a critical stance when faced with an enthusiastic source who touts a new intervention as "promising" and "interesting."

1. Natural course?

Many diseases, including infections, have a good prognosis. They usually heal even without treatment—if you only wait long enough. These conditions are self-limiting, and the body's recuperative processes are strong enough to fight off the disease. Even diseases that are potentially life-threatening and "incurable" may occasionally heal without any medical intervention whatsoever. Chronic diseases may vary in intensity from one time to another. Their natural course may be cyclical—sometimes the condition gets worse, sometimes better. This is true for certain rheumatic and allergic conditions, multiple sclerosis, and many gastrointestinal conditions. This means that a treatment that is started in a phase of remission can seem effective, even if it has no effect at all. Clinical trials should use a control group of patients with the same condition to be able to attribute improvements to the treatment.

2. Wishful thinking?

Any strong conviction affects our perception of reality. If the stakes are high, our conviction can be very strong indeed. A treatment that initially seems effective to those who pioneer in testing it may later turn out to have no measurable effect on life span or quality of life. The commitment of time, money, and prestige to the new intervention may have been so great that it is impossible for those involved to accept that it is ineffective. The enthusiastic researcher/entrepreneur, the caring health professional, and the hopeful patient may want to interpret reality differently. To avoid a painful insight, they engage in wishful thinking. When the treatment is eventually tested in an unbiased context where the stakes are lower, it may prove ineffective.

3. Caring effect?

Health care is much more than medical interventions. It includes many other ways of caring for the patient. Nursing, comforting, and supporting the patient can have powerful effects on health and quality of life. Sometimes these interventions are not taken into account, and their effects may be hard to distinguish from the effects of medical interventions. For example, when new treatments are tried out, patients may be followed more closely than otherwise. Extra time and effort may be devoted to the patients who are participating in a study since it is particularly important to monitor the effects of the treatment and to encourage patients to comply with the protocol. Hence, it is not unlikely that these patients are offered more frequent appointments and longer visits than normal. Special counseling and social support might help patients experience fewer symptoms or interpret them differently. Such caring effects can be mistaken for treatment effects.

4. Placebo effect?

Medical interventions are usually expected to be effective. Patients, researchers, and clinicians assume that treatments will do more good than harm. Thanks to such assumptions, even sham treatments may affect the course of a disease. Patients may suffer fewer symptoms. To distinguish these effects from the more specific effects of an intervention, it is generally recommended that clinical trials give a placebo to the control group when possible and ethically acceptable. The subjects do not know whether they are offered the real treatment or a placebo.

WHAT ARE THE SACRIFICES?

Enthusiasts tend to forget that everything has its price. Media audiences can be grossly misled by enthusiastic experts who focus on potential (often short-term) benefits and forget about the (often long-term) risks (e.g., side effects) and costs. Or, conversely, alarmists can mislead by discussing only the drawbacks. Therefore, benefits, risks, and costs should all be considered.

Weighing pros and cons, costs and benefits, is key in all decision making, whether by patients, health professionals, or policymakers. Tools for making these calculations explicit are provided by the discipline called *health economics*. To health economists, a *benefit* is what is gained by meeting a need we choose to meet. *Costs* are the sacrifices we make by meeting that need (i.e., by forgoing the benefits we would have gained by using resources differently).

Like all economic logic, the logic of health economics is based on the notion of *scarcity*. Resources are scarce. *Resources* include time, staff, buildings, equipment, and capital. Since money is used to trade resources and services, the term *resources* is commonly used as a synonym for *money*.

Needs must be met by limited resources. A basic principle is that every decision to use resources implies a *sacrifice*. Once resources are used in one way, they cannot be used in another manner. Most people are painfully aware that hospital treatment requires sacrifices. They pay a price not only in money but also in time and energy—resources that they could have used differently.

Choosing a different sort of treatment, or avoiding treatment altogether, is associated with other benefits and different costs. To obtain as much benefit as possible for as low a cost as possible, resources must be spent wisely. Costs and benefits of different alternatives need to be weighed against each other. This is the aim of economic evaluation. Health economics enhances the decision-making process through valuating and explicitly describing the balance between costs and benefits. It clarifies choices.

Although both cost and quality are considered, economic evaluation does not automatically identify a single best solution. It can only suggest which way is most cost-effective in achieving a certain goal or describe the effects of alternative actions. In addition to cost-effectiveness, decision makers need to consider ethical aspects, social justice, and political imperatives. Journalists can provide their audiences with useful information if they include these aspects in addition to economic benefits and costs.

Four types of health-economic analyses are commonly used by health economists:

1. *Cost-minimization analysis* is a method used when the effects of different interventions are the same. It aims to identify which alternative means the lowest cost.
2. *Cost-effectiveness analysis* is used when the effects of different interventions may vary but are still measurable in identical and natural units (e.g., years of life saved).
3. *Cost-utility analysis* measures effects in utilities, units that have been constructed to include not only years of life but also quality of life (e.g., quality-adjusted life-years, QALYs). Costs per unit of utility (e.g., cost per QALY) are compared for different interventions.
4. *Cost-benefit analysis* attempts to translate both costs and benefits to money, supposedly making it easier to compare different sectors of society.

Debates on national health care budgets can easily convey the impression that expenditures for health services only burden the national economy without yielding any returns. However, health services also contribute to employment, industrial development, and industrial growth.[127] Reporters may consider how health services contribute to a nation's overall economy, maintain the health of productive individuals in society, influence the amount of sick leave taken and early retirement, and contribute to the trade of medical goods and the industrial development of pharmaceuticals and medical equipment.

INTERVIEWING PATIENTS AND THEIR FAMILIES

It should not need to be said that the patient is health care's raison d'être. Health care's mission is neither scientific nor economic—it is humanitarian. If health services fail to

No, you idiot! When I said the patient is fighting for air, I meant oxygen.

help patients, they do not accomplish their primary goal. One of the most important tasks for medical reporters is to give a voice to users of health services. The personal stories of patients and their families bring life and meaning to medical reporting. These stories can be powerful and should be reported with great care. The journalist's task is to report fairly and accurately and to choose cases accordingly. If the examples chosen are likely to confuse or mislead the audience, the reporter has done a poor job.

From an ethical point of view, interviewing a patient suffering from serious disease can, in the acute stage, be compared to interviewing a victim of war, crime, or natural disaster. The interviewee may be in a state of shock and severe distress, which may last long after the interview. Furthermore, being ill may entail losing one's sense of control and judgment. Patients and their families may be so vulnerable that they agree to media coverage without fully realizing the consequences of being the focus of public attention. Journalistic codes of conduct require that reporters should always show the greatest possible consideration for patients and their families and refrain from abusing their vulnerability in pursuit of a good story.

CHAPTER 5

Pitfalls in Medical Reporting

> When stories on the latest laparoscope, laser, or lithotriptor outnumber stories on issues concerning health policy, access to care, and quality of care, something is out of balance.
>
> —Gary Schwitzer, formerly medical news producer–correspondent for CNN

> To be frank, I'm a bit disheartened by the current trends in medical journalism—the scoop mentality, the "infotainment" angle to health stories, and the pressure to cover stories that are preliminary or insignificant, in response to corporate demand or, more sadly, to keep up with the Joneses in the media itself.
>
> —Sarah Masters, vice president and editor-in-chief, Reuters Health Information

Chapter objectives
- **Suggest how the validity of medical claims can be checked**
- **Discuss the importance of identifying appropriate expert sources**
- **Highlight differences between anecdotes and systematic research**
- **Point out that poor research gets published in medical journals**
- **Explain why surrogate outcomes can be deceptive**
- **Distinguish statistical significance from clinical significance**
- **Explain the difference between risk factors and disease, and suggest how health risks can be compared**

There are many possible ways in which the media can approach a given medical topic. Depending on the type of medium and its particular constraints and policies, some reports will be more informative than others. They will emphasize different aspects, reporting different sides to a story that complete or contradict each other. This is how the media are supposed to work.

However, regardless of setting, a general commitment to fair and accurate reporting is expected from all journalists who report news to the public. Such a commitment is expressed in journalists' professional codes of ethics (see chapter 6). This distinguishes journalism from such other professions as fiction writing, entertainment, and marketing. Fiction writers, entertainers, and marketing managers do not share journalists' responsibility to "seek truth and report it" and to "test the accuracy of information from all sources and exercise care to avoid inadvertent error," as the U.S. Society of Professional Journalists puts it.[187]

The following list of pitfalls in medical reporting is not intended to be comprehensive. It aims to provide examples of difficulties that are often encountered in medical journalism and that reporters should be aware of. Avoiding some of them should be possible and would accord with the journalistic mission to be critical of sources.

PITFALL 1: REDUCING REPORTING TO QUOTING

If reporters do not ask experts for evidence supporting their claims or check the claims' veracity in other ways, the message conveyed to the audience may be untrue even though the experts' quotes are technically accurate.[128] Truthful reporting is thereby reduced to quoting accurately something that has been said, without checking whether what has been said is true.[14]

To avoid acting as a megaphone for seriously misleading health information, reporters sometimes seek verification from two or three independent experts who can agree that a statement is correct.[128] However, reporters should always remain skeptical of authoritative statements.[129] One important reason is that experts' recommendations have been shown to lag behind empirical evidence.[130]

Credible sources have firsthand knowledge of the topic and are often able to verify their statements. However, when a source cannot provide evidence to verify important statements, the thorough journalist searches for it elsewhere. A wealth of background information is available in reference books and—of course—on the Internet. A concise, useful, and regularly updated summary compendium called Clinical Evidence covers the treatment and prevention of a wide range of clinical conditions and summarizes the best available scientific evidence based on extensive literature searches (for further information, see http://www.evidence.org). *Best Evidence*, currently published on CD-ROM, is a compilation of thousands of abstracts from two journals (*ACP Journal Club* and *Evidence-Based Medicine*). These two journals review, rate the quality of, and summarize new and important clinical studies published by other journals. More high-quality information can be found at the Cochrane Library Website (http://www.update-software.com/cochrane/cochrane-frame.html), at the Cochrane Collaboration Website (http://hiru.mcmaster.ca/cochrane/default.htm), and in a compilation of Web resources called Netting the Evidence (http://www.shef.ac.uk/uni/academic/R-Z/scharr/ir/netting.html), produced by the School of Health and Related Research at the University of Sheffield, United Kingdom. In special cases, and for results of basic research, reporters may want to search MEDLINE and other biomedical databases via the Internet (http://www.nlm.nih.gov/hinfo.html) or at medical libraries. If a reporter remains uncertain of the information's accuracy after trying to verify it, this should be made clear to the public.

Experienced medical reporters ask about large-scale clinical trials when they face sources who use preliminary findings to promote new treatments. Such reporters are also aware that unblinded or nonrandomized studies are less reliable than blinded or randomized ones, distinctions that the public does not always understand.[131]

Both experts' *opinions* and scientific *findings* are relevant in medical stories. Both should be reported. However, they are not interchangeable. For example, a scientific study can compare the effects of a new health policy with an old one, but there may be different opinions about which effects are the most desirable. A news story should make it possible for the audience to distinguish between opinions and evidence. When experts seem to ignore scientific findings, can they give a good reason for doing so? Are the research results in question unreliable, and if so, why? The audience should be told whether or not an expert statement about the effects of a certain treatment is supported (or contradicted) by solid evidence. Are sources withholding important information?

One medical reporter puts it succinctly: "Many people are out there trying to sell their snake oil and their high-priced antihypertensive drug that probably have no advantages and may have a whole bunch of disadvantages. What they will tell you is that it's the latest thing, it's much better than anything else, it's the cat's meow. Those of us [journalists] who just report what they tell us are nothing but hacks, flaks, and lackeys."[67]

PITFALL 2: TREATING SPECIALISTS AS GENERALISTS

A golden rule of journalism is to know your sources. In particular, reporters must identify expert sources' particular field of expertise. Leading experts in certain fields sometimes like to think that their excellence spills over into other areas, making them experts in many other fields as well. An appetite for publicity may contribute to such misperceptions. Reporters should not lead their audiences astray by letting an expert's feelings of omnipotence run rampant.[132]

For example, the inexperienced reporter may assume that an expert on cell proliferation also knows about cancer treatment, when in fact he or she may be completely ignorant in this related field. This is particularly problematic in a vast area like medicine, which has developed so many subdisciplines and sub-subdisciplines. An expert on laboratory cancer studies may be ignorant when it comes to treating cancer in clinical practice, and vice versa. An expert on breast cancer may be ignorant about rectal cancer, and so on.

To sum up, experts are not experts outside their own particular field. Their seemingly authoritative statements about other topics are likely to arise from speculation, prejudice, or delusion. It is up to journalists to find out enough about the experts to judge their credibility, analyze their arguments, and ask probing questions. Experts should be able to substantiate their statements with solid facts, theoretical support, internal consistency, and logic.

The problem of determining an expert's credibility is not unique to journalism. It becomes a problem for the courts as well when trial lawyers hire experts to testify on scientific matters. The difficulty in evaluating expert testimony in American courtrooms was the topic of a 1997 National Public Radio report entitled "Expert for Hire."[133] According to this report, critics claim that questionable science is invited into the courtroom. The report goes on to explain how the scientific process can get lost in the adversarial process of justice, and the reporter observes that "there is an entire industry built around finding courtroom experts to argue anyone's case."

Rather than succumbing to the temptation to simply contrast two different expert opinions, medical journalists may scan systematic reviews of the best available research evidence on a topic. Much of the information that answers key questions has already been tracked down, critically appraised, and packaged in easily accessible forms. Systematic reviews are easy to find on the Internet, for example, in the Cochrane Library. Medical journalists looking for relevant expert judgment should also ascertain, by checking credentials, that the persons referred to as experts actually have in-depth knowledge of the field in question.

PITFALL 3: CONFUSING SCIENCE FICTION WITH SCIENTIFIC FACTS

Public expectations about what health care and medical technology can achieve in curing disease and relieving symptoms are sometimes unrealistically high. Not only patients and their families but scientists and health professionals who share these high expectations can be led astray. For instance, we often wrongly assume that new treatments are better than established ones. When new, "promising" technologies emerge, shared hopes among clinicians and researchers may lead to wishful thinking. The media's quest for breakthrough news may reinforce this tendency, which, in turn, creates media hype that bolsters patients' unrealistic expectations. Examples of such misleading health promises in the media—promises that may or may not have been withdrawn in later reports—are legion.

For instance, in the early years of the AIDS epidemic, network news coverage of potential cures for the syndrome was misleading, and hopeful expert statements were never revised when the treatments proved to be failures.[48] The clinical application of gene therapies has been heavily promoted in the media, although important technical problems remain. Success in the ability to diagnose and predict genetic disease does not imply the availability of therapeutic solutions. Promises of therapeutic solutions are likely to be premature.[134] Other examples of early hype include an unusual and invasive treatment for Alzheimer's disease, an intervention that was widely publicized after a small, unblinded pilot study;[135] the hormone melatonin, which received excessively positive early media coverage as a "cure" for aging;[83,136-37] and Celebrex, a new pain-relieving drug that was widely reported without regard to the unknowns, the potential downsides, or the financial ties of information sources.[138]

Generally, medical publications that have not been peer-reviewed, including conference reports and supplements to scientific journals, are more likely to be biased than others.[139] For example, in a comparison of drug articles that had been peer-reviewed with those that had not, the authors show that the nonreviewed articles more often concern a single drug, have a misleading title, and mention commercial drugs by name.[140] Compared with the literature that has gone through peer review, considerably fewer of the conference reports that deal with passive smoking show that it has some adverse effects on health.[141–42] Similarly, symposium articles are also less likely to disclose their source of funding, and more likely to be written by tobacco-industry-affiliated authors, than peer-reviewed journal articles.

Critical medical reporters are wary of vested interests such as the commercial interests that often lie behind overly optimistic medical claims. However, as Lawrence Altman of the *New York Times* points out, conflicts of interest are common even outside industry: "There is an underlying assumption that if something is done by industry, you've got to be very suspicious; it's probably wrong. And if something is done by government or NIH [National Institutes of Health], it's probably right. It's totally inconsistent to me. The criteria should be applied equally on either side."[16]

Ignoring vested interests—whether commercial or noncommercial—and playing along with enthusiastic, biased sources undermine journalistic credibility. Expert opinion can only complement—not replace—results from reliable clinical trials. After all, scientific facts are not established by authorities' opinions but by systematic research.

PITFALL 4: BEING MISLED BY NUMBER GAMES

One of the rhetorical devices that sources occasionally employ is emphasizing a statement's objectivity and accuracy by using *excessive precision* in numbers. In some scientific contexts, an answer is not considered a real answer unless it is numerical,[143] and this axiom is sometimes taken to extremes. Inexperienced media workers might play along. For example, when a source states that the incidence of a particular condition is 27.3 percent, the reporter may fail to note that the entire study included only eleven subjects, and the condition was found in three. While the calculation itself is correct (3/11 = 27.272727), the precision used is deceptively high. A less misleading way to describe this result might be "approximately one in four."

Another number game sources often play is the *relative risk reduction*. In this play, sources will refer to relative figures—for instance, "the new treatment cuts the risk for stroke by one-third"—that sound impressive.[144] They will fail to mention that the risk was rather low in the first place, for example, that the reduction in this instance was really only from 3 percent to 2 percent. The rule of thumb for medical reporters is that no percentage means much unless you know the base on which the percentage was calculated. The critical medical reporter asks for NNT, *number needed to treat,* which gives a more realistic picture of the clinical trade-offs involved.[145]

NNT is the number of patients you need to treat to prevent one bad outcome (death, stroke, and the like) that would otherwise occur. How is NNT calculated? First, you have to identify the risk without treatment and the risk with treatment. The difference between these is the absolute reduction of risk. NNT is the inverse of that number. The absolute benefit in the above example is $3 - 2 = 1$ percentage unit, or 0.01. To calculate NNT: $1/0.01 = 100$. It means that 100 patients must be treated to prevent one event. If the absolute risk reduction had been even smaller, say, 0.3 percentage units, or 0.003, then NNT would be higher, $1/0.003 = 333$. (NNTs are always rounded up to the nearest whole number.) In this case, the NNT shows that 333 patients must be treated to obtain the desired effect in one patient.

Inexperienced or gullible reporters may parrot relative risk reductions without reporting absolute numbers and thereby mislead their audiences. In a study from Harvard Medical School,[261] researchers analyzed media coverage of three different drugs in a sample of 207 stories featured in television and newspapers between 1994 and 1998. Of the 124 stories that quantified benefits, 103 (83 percent) used relative framing of risks. Three percent of the stories analyzed used absolute numbers, and 14 percent used both absolute numbers and relative figures, which gives readers the best chance of assessing the importance of the information.

The message is: Do not accept benefits (or risks) expressed as percentages unless you also know the absolute numbers. Simple percentages may mislead the audience.[144] A large percentage risk reduction may have little relevance when the initial risk is small. Conversely, even a small percentage reduction can be highly significant when the initial risk is large.

PITFALL 5: DEPENDING ON ANECDOTES FOR EVIDENCE

Single success stories or dramatic failures *(anecdotal evidence)* are often cited by the media. However, experienced medical reporters use them selectively as a narrative technique and do not confuse them with scientific evidence. Philip Meyer, veteran reporter and professor of journalism at the University of North Carolina at Chapel Hill, writes: "We are overly susceptible to anecdotal evidence. Anecdotes make good reading and we are right to use them. . . . But we often forget to remind our readers—and ourselves— of the folly of generalizing from a few interesting cases. . . . The statistic is hard to remember. The stories are not."[114] For science journalists who want to be their readers' advocates, it is crucial to be skeptical of anecdotes. Faced with isolated stories of medical success or failure, they will ask: "Does this apply to my audience? Are the claims justified, or are they based on a biased or unrepresentative sample?"

Single-subject studies are vulnerable to all kinds of biases that make generalization very difficult or impossible. The results of all single-subject studies are bound to have this problem to one extent or another. Without population statistics, there is—as a rule—no way of knowing with any certainty whether the results apply to other people or just to this person, and whether the results are due to chance alone. Analyses cannot be done on a sample of one. General conclusions may be drawn from larger samples by "averaging out" the superficial differences among individual cases to see what meaningful similarities remain (which may represent the effects of a medical treatment).[146]

Statistics are almost always needed to accurately assess the effects of a treatment. As statistician Dr. Robert Hooke notes: "Edison had it easy. It doesn't take statistics to see that a light has come on."[147] There are of course interventions so effective or so necessary that their utility is indisputable. That stopping heavy bleeding prevents death need not be confirmed by randomized controlled trials. However, the history of medicine shows that such self-evident valid treatments should be regarded as rare exceptions.[148-50] Recent demands for a more solid scientific basis for clinical practice—the quest for evidence-based health care—have been described as announcing a paradigm shift in medicine.[151-52] Some of its proponents hypothesize that the systematic use of large-scale randomized evidence could prevent hundreds of thousands of premature deaths worldwide.[153]

Journalists' predilection for anecdotes is not a problem if they use such narrative devices judiciously. Anecdotes breathe life into medical stories, create empathy, and help the audience understand an individual patient's situation. Although single cases may *illustrate* the effects of a treatment, anecdotes should never be portrayed as *evidence*. The journalist must actively help the audience understand that high-powered scientific studies, such as many large randomized clinical trials, are the only way to get reliable and generally applicable results when it comes to measuring and comparing the effectiveness of different treatments. Medical journalists who use anecdotes as a narrative technique in such contexts should search for typical, rather than atypical, cases.

In the drive to detect an intervention's rare but important side effects, single cases provide scientists with crucial bits of a complex puzzle. Each case is analyzed with great care to exclude other possible explanations for anomalies. For journalists, it is tempting to jump to conclusions about adverse effects. In a candid background paper, *New York Times* science reporter Gina Kolata describes this temptation as "the tyranny of the anecdote." Describing a story she had written about a woman with a leaking silicone breast implant and how that could be related to a life-threatening autoimmune disorder that hit the woman, Kolata explains: "But it seemed so clear. The devices leaked and ruptured—that had been well known for decades. It couldn't be good for you to have silicone spilling into your body." In retrospect, however, she observes:

> Yet my assumptions turned out to be wrong. After the FDA and the Justice Department investigated and combed through the company's files, both cleared Dow Corning of hiding anything of substance from the FDA. And when there finally was a body of published scientific reports asking whether women who had implants were more likely to develop any of a variety of diseases, virtually every well-conducted study failed to find that women with implants were at any greater risk than women without them.[154]

Discussing how to avoid jumping to faulty conclusions as a medical reporter, Kolata comments:

> The first problem is to recognize what is, and what is not, evidence. Yes, I was swayed by Maria Stern's story. She had implants, they leaked, she became ill. But I recognized that I was falling prey to what I call the tyranny of the anecdote. . . . One clue to assessing this evidence is to ask whether the studies were published and, if so, whether they were published in major medical journals. After all, compelling and credible evidence that implants cause disease is pretty shattering. A well-done study should be publishable in a journal like the *New England Journal of Medicine* or the *Journal of the American Medical Association*. . . . [R]eporters can best serve their readers by being wary of the tyranny of the anecdote, by seeking out and questioning disinterested experts, by always asking, and reporting, potential sources of bias, and by keeping an open mind and realizing that our gut feelings may not reflect the truth.[154]

PITFALL 6: FAILING TO QUESTION FINDINGS ABOUT A TREATMENT'S EFFECTS

Clinical trials do not deliver definite truths about a treatment's effects, though experts sometimes claim they do. All research results are more or less uncertain. At best, clinical trials can deliver a fairly accurate picture of a treatment's effects. At worst, they can be so biased and flawed that the results are invalid and the conclusions utterly false. Results from a single study rarely prove anything. Findings should be replicated by different researchers to be considered solid. As every experienced medical reporter knows, there is no guarantee that published studies are reliable—far from it. Though peer-reviewed articles are generally less biased that nonreviewed articles, even highly unreliable results can be published in peer-reviewed scientific journals. In a randomized controlled trial looking at peer review, a paper with eight significant errors was sent to 420 reviewers in *JAMA*'s database. None spotted more than five errors, and most not more than two.[155]

According to medical reporter Lawrence Altman of the *New York Times*, the peer-review system, which is generally regarded as a safeguard against scientific flaws, is overrated by health professionals. "The weaknesses and flaws of the peer-review process are rarely discussed," says Dr. Altman, who is also clinical associate professor of medicine at New York University Medical School. "I am amazed at the lack of critical thinking about a topic that many doctors take almost as religious dogma."[156]

Altman notes that medical journals not only represent scholarship. They are also an industry, which benefits, like other media, from advertising revenues. The economic aspects of scientific publication, and the fact that journals strive for increased readership and circulation, are reflected in their efforts to promote their products to news reporters:

Today we get tons of news releases from medical journals. They call us and push their own products like any other commercial enterprise would. This is new. The biggest journals may have done it for some years now. But now everyone does it, even the Journal of the Left Toe. I am not saying it is wrong. You just have to be cautious as a medical journalist what you choose. Some of these journals don't even send you the journal itself, just the release. As journalists, we should be critical readers of data and information. We should not just accept what are in essence handouts from medical journals, because that would simply be lazy journalism. [156]

Even some journals are critical of their own press activities. A public-relations officer (who asked to remain anonymous) at a major international medical journal says:

Personally, I think we should stop producing these news releases. They don't provide the necessary caveats and context that we claim are so important. Instead of emphasizing the most important issues, they hype the "newsiest" ones. Nor are they confined to peer-reviewed material only but occasionally refer to letters, editorials, and commentaries. Yet, many journalists take them for gospel. There is no need for this anymore. Journalists should go to the primary sources.

A basic understanding of research methodology and an elementary knowledge of the most common errors in clinical research are essential for journalists working with medical news. (See chapter 3.) Even when the proper research methods have been used, including a sufficient number of observations over a sufficiently long period, critical reporters always find out what category of patients has actually been studied. This tells them what sort of patients the results actually apply to, and under what circumstances.

PITFALL 7: EXTRAPOLATING FROM RESEARCH TO CLINICAL PRACTICE

Researchers often need to isolate the effects of treatment to clearly identify a cause-and-effect relationship. Therein lies a problem. They may create such a special research situation that their study, even if well executed and randomized, no longer corresponds to everyday clinical practice. Patient selection and protocols may be so narrow that they correspond only to exceptional situations and not to clinical reality. If, for example, a large randomized study shows that a treatment is effective in childless women over age fifty, we cannot assume that it will be similarly effective in other groups of women. But these others may, in fact, be the typical patients.

Analysts often distinguish between "efficacy," the results of a treatment (or a diagnostic method) used under ideal conditions in a study, and "effectiveness," the results of the same method deployed in routine clinical practice. The difference between

I do understand that you need breaking news but I repeat: None of our laboratory rats is willing to talk to the press about their new treatment!

efficacy and effectiveness is often substantial. Hence, new treatments must also be studied in everyday clinical settings before we know how well they actually work.

Some extrapolation is unavoidable. It is impossible to require scientific evidence for all conceivable indications in all patient groups before adopting a new treatment. For various reasons, pregnant women, newborns, and the elderly are seldom included in research that informs decisions about adopting a new method of care. The patients that a physician meets on a daily basis are not as homogeneous a group as research subjects who participate in studies. Even the symptoms of a particular illness may vary more in clinical practice than in research studies.

However, it is impossible—and in some instances morally indefensible—to limit the use of a new treatment or technology strictly to the groups that have been studied in research projects. Some expanded application must be accepted. What should be avoided is an uncontrolled proliferation of new and untested interventions, which makes it impossible to differentiate treatment effects from random events.[157]

Research findings showing that a method is effective against a particular disease inspire hope that the method can be used to effectively treat other, similar diseases. But serious problems can arise when a treatment that works against one disease is assumed to work against others. Applying such a treatment more broadly may be directly harmful. New indications usually require new studies.

PITFALL 8: HYPING A STUDY'S CLINICAL IMPLICATIONS

Many results that are statistically significant are completely irrelevant and useless in real-life clinical practice. For example, to most men with benign prostate enlargement, it is irrelevant that a certain treatment reduces the measurable volume of the gland in a statistically significant way. The interesting question for them is whether the treatment relieves symptoms, which is why they would want treatment in the first place.

In many clinical trials, researchers use only indirect measures of benefit or harm. Instead of measuring "real" clinical end points—such as quality of life, symptoms, or death, that is to say, tangible benefit or harm—they use so-called surrogate end points. These are more or less closely associated with the real end point. Surrogate variables may be easier and less resource-consuming to measure. In fact, surrogate end points may be the only acceptable option if it would be too invasive, harmful, or unethical to measure the true outcome.

Nevertheless, the results of studies using surrogate end points do not necessarily reflect the real outcomes. For example, a researcher who wants to evaluate the benefits of a cytotoxic drug against cancer may choose reduction of tumor volume as an end point instead of increased survival rate or prolonged survival. Even if the drug is effective in reducing the tumor volume, it may be so toxic that its adverse effects kill the patient. The most extreme example, of course, is the gruesome joke about the surgeon who says, "The operation was successful but the patient died."

In the early 1990s, the world witnessed a drastic example of the deadly effects that relying on surrogate end points can have. A team of researchers carried out a randomized controlled study of the benefits of giving the drugs encainide, flecainide, and moricizine to patients who have suffered an acute myocardial infarction, using ventricular arrhythmia as an end point.[158] The rationale was that death in such patients is commonly caused by ventricular fibrillation, induced by ventricular arrhythmia. The study showed that these drugs were more effective than a placebo in treating ventricular arrhythmia. Hence, it was believed that such medication is effective and should be used. Encainide, flecainide, and moricizine were shortly thereafter approved by the Food and Drug Administration (FDA) for use in patients with life-threatening or severely symptomatic arrhythmias. More than 200,000 people eventually took these drugs in one year in the United States alone, although no follow-up trials had been done to determine if the treatment actually saved lives.[159] If such studies had been available, they would have shown that not only did these drugs not *save* lives—they even killed patients. The mortality in the intervention group would have been higher than in the placebo group. When a mortality study was eventually begun, it had to be stopped because the treatment group's death rate was so much higher than the control group's.[160]

This is a prime example of how badly intermediate, surrogate, or proxy outcomes may work as substitutes for the actual treatment target. They are sometimes completely misleading, and assessments based on surrogate measures are likely to be less reliable.[161] In particular, overreliance on proxy or surrogate outcomes has fueled vain hopes for various health technologies. Examples include medical treatment of ocular glaucoma (where pressure inside the eye was used as a surrogate for visual-field damage), interferon against chronic hepatitis (where normalized markers of viral replication, or liver enzymes, were used as surrogates for hepatic failure and death), anti-osteoporotic drugs (where bone mineral content was used as a surrogate for fractures), and zidovudine for AIDS patients (where lymphocyte helper count was used as a surrogate for survival).[162]

There are many problems involved with using surrogate end points, and there is no simple remedy. A *British Medical Journal* article points out other dangerous pitfalls related to surrogate measures,[163] and readers who want to know more should consult it. A change in a surrogate end point cannot in and of itself demonstrate what is the best available treatment for a particular condition. Relying on a single surrogate end point as a measure of therapeutic success usually reflects an extremely narrow clinical perspective. Moreover, surrogate measures are often developed in animal models of disease, which means that extrapolations to humans may well be invalid.

Used inappropriately, surrogate end points lead to faulty, even deadly, decisions. Some authors suggest that results obtained with surrogates should be regarded as preliminary.[161] Critical medical reporters will be aware of this and should ask about large, definitive trials with clinically relevant outcomes. Noting in their reports the need for such trials will enhance their stories' journalistic quality.

The top priority for medical reporters is to ask questions that their audience would want answered. However, this is not always what the interviewed experts want to discuss. One reason is that research does not always address the questions most pertinent to the public, in which case the researchers cannot provide reliable answers. According to Hilda Bastian, Australian consumer activist in the scientific network Cochrane Collaboration, it is hard for medical experts to see what is most important from a patient's perspective:

> Researchers can limit their studies to certain aspects of treatment outcome, to surrogate measures like tumor volume, blood tests, etc. The patient is probably more concerned with how the disease will affect his or her daily life. For example, many patients want to know more about long-term effects of treatments, including quality of life. Today, researchers focus more on aspects that they can observe themselves and less on what patients experience outside hospitals and clinics.[164]

Animal studies, commonly referred to by drug companies in marketing campaigns, are particularly problematic. Results from animal studies are often used by companies as arguments for human applications of the same drugs. However, medical reporters must be aware that the researchers have created an experimental situation for animals that may be irrelevant for human beings.

Four main problems arise in interpretations of the results of animal studies:[165]

1. Selection of species: Different species of animal can yield different research results.
2. Lack of physiological comparability between animals and human beings: Many differences between animal and human physiology, only some of which have been discovered, can lead to misinterpretations.
3. Differences in appropriate drug doses in animals and human beings.
4. Measurement and interpretation of pain or psychological effects are difficult or impossible in animal studies. Attempting to interpret changed behavior in animals is a risky enterprise too.

Not even a treatment's most obvious effects will necessarily be the same in human beings and animals. The most catastrophic example of this fact is thalidomide, which in human females—but not in female animals—forms a substance that maims a developing fetus. Another example is a substance used to treat arteriosclerosis that increased the mortality rate in human subjects. However, no such increase was seen in animal studies.

The journalistic approach must be consumer-oriented when the general public is the target audience. Lawrence Altman of the *New York Times* enlarges on this point: "When I write an article, I try to think of the reader as a patient, as personally concerned with information important to some acknowledged need. I try to anticipate what the patient/reader wants to know and what questions he or she might ask."[166]

PITFALL 9: MISTAKING RISK FACTORS FOR DISEASES

Medical research continues to uncover new risk factors all the time. These are, for example, particular patient characteristics that are associated with a higher probability of disease. Sometimes—but not always—such factors are also *causally* linked to a certain disease. Yet people often assume that risk factors always call for treatment and that treatment will automatically lower the risk for disease. Both of these assumptions may be wrong.

A risk factor is not an illness in itself but a signal. Treating a warning signal does not necessarily deflect an oncoming disease, and it may even be harmful. What's more, many people who belong to an at-risk population will never develop the disease that they are at risk for. Therefore, medical reporters need to be aware of the difficulties of distinguishing between risk factors and diseases.

High blood pressure, for example, can be a serious health risk. However, according to a systematic review of the scientific literature, if blood pressure is only mildly elevated, and if the patient is young and has no symptoms or signs of organ involvement, the benefits of treatment are modest.[167-68] More specifically, treatment of healthy people between thirty-five and fifty-four who have only mild hypertension and show no signs or symptoms of organ involvement increases their chances of avoiding cardiovascular disease and stroke from 99.3 percent to 99.6 percent.[167-68] Thus, it has been suggested that in such cases, the elevated blood pressure should be regarded as a risk factor, not a disease.

One of the authors of the review, Dr. Kurt Svärdsudd of Uppsala University in Sweden, comments: "These figures from the SBU [Swedish Council on Technology Assessment in Health Care] report illustrate that we should not start treating large population groups before we are certain that interventions offer greater benefit than harm." Discussing risk factors in general, Dr. Svärdsudd points out that the presence of a single factor is seldom serious: "A minority of those with only one disease warning signal will actually become ill. A single risk factor probably increases the risk for disease by only a few percentage points."[169] A combination of several risk factors is usually needed for disease to appear.

Factors that appear more often in people with a particular disease are not necessarily the root cause of that disease. Underlying conditions may cause both the risk factor and the disease. Dr. Svärdsudd gives an example. "People with red hair have more surgery-related problems than non-redheads. Having red hair may be a small risk factor, but naturally it is not a cause."[169]

Since risk factors do not necessarily cause disease, it is uncertain whether interventions to reduce them will prevent disease. Thus, medical interventions against risk factors sometimes do more harm than good. As in the case of treatment for disease, critical medical reporters ask for evidence that an intervention against risk factors actually benefits the patient.

PITFALL 10: MISJUDGING RISKS

Risk researchers study how people perceive potentially harmful situations and describe the complexity of our risk perceptions. Many factors, apart from the statistical odds, influence our perceptions. For example, we tend to consider rare but dramatic events to be greater hazards than the familiar risks that we face every day. Furthermore, our tolerance is greater for risks that we ourselves have decided to take than for those that are imposed on us by others. Considering such variations, it is easy to see why it is hard to pinpoint the potential benefits and costs of avoiding various health risks. Although many of these stories are covered by environmental reporters, rather than medical journalists, some aspects of risk reporting will be discussed here.

Risk research suggests that most of us think about threats the same way we experience noise or heat—in a personal way. Therefore, measurements of decibels or degrees Fahrenheit do not always fit in with our perceptions. We base our interpretations of the environment on knowledge, emotions, and personal experiences. Our ranking of risks is also associated with the attention given to them in the media. Fair risk reporting tries not only to catch the audience's attention but also to give them a realistic idea of the actual odds involved.

It's for you Mike. The master cook at the Ritz is preparing tomorrow's menu and wants to know what particular food we are going to call a "potential health hazard" tonight.

Providing accurate risk estimates can be a real challenge to reporters. Experts often come to different conclusions, partly due to methodological problems. The same data may be evaluated differently by different scientists.

Communicating scientists' findings in a meaningful way can also be a problem for reporters. Research has shown that it is hard for people who are not scientists to grasp risk magnitudes in terms of numerical odds or probabilities.[170] Part of the explanation may be that the range is so wide—from the greater than 1 in 10 risk that we will eventually die of cancer to the less than 1 in 10 million chance of being killed by lightning in any one year.[171] The range between such extremes is, indeed, unfathomable.

Some risk researchers have suggested that risks should be shown on a logarithmic scale.[172–73] In contrast to reporting precise probabilities, such a scale would reflect the fact that risk research generally deals with orders of magnitude rather than exact numbers. A log scale like the one in table 5.1 would help people assess spurious precision.[171] A log scale is even more useful if other ways of expressing risk are combined with it.[171] Thus, table 5.1 classifies risks according to the size of human communities: for example, a street with around 100 inhabitants, a small town of 10,000, and a large country of 100,000,000 serve as frames of reference. These comparisons are, of course, only rough estimates. For example, a street can be smaller or larger. Nevertheless, this table provides a frame of reference for journalists who want to put risk magnitudes in perspective for their audience.

A source of further confusion related to health risks is that it is impossible to scientifically prove that two factors are unrelated. In other words, no study can ever show

Table 5.1. Logarithmic risk scale and community risk description (reprinted with permission) [171]

Risk	Risk magnitude	Community risk description (unit in which one adverse event would be expected)	Example (based on number of deaths per year in Great Britain)
1 in 1	10	Person	
1 in 10	9	Family	
1 in 100	8	Street	Any cause
1 in 1,000	7	Village	Any cause, at age 40
1 in 10,000	6	Small town	Road accident
1 in 100,000	5	Large town	Murder
1 in 1,000,000	4	City	Oral contraceptives
1 in 10,000,000	3	Province or country	Lightning
1 in 100,000,000	2	Large country	Measles
1 in 1,000,000,000	1	Continent	
1 in 10,000,000,000	0	World	

with 100 percent certainty that something is *not* harmful.[129] Moreover, the associations found between an exposure and a disease may originate from animal studies, historical data, cohort studies, or case control studies, all with their particular methodological strengths and weaknesses.

Media reports about health risks should tell who is exposed and try to include the odds for those people. Providing comparisons may help the audience decide how serious a particular risk really is. Failing to do so may provoke unnecessary alarm or lead to false reassurance.

CHAPTER 6

Critical Medical Journalism

A reporter, without being cynical and believing nothing, should be . . . skeptical and greet every claim by saying, in words or thought: Show me.
—Victor Cohn, science and medical reporter for the *Washington Post*

If your doctor does not think it is good for you to sleep, to drink wine, or eat of a particular dish, do not worry; I will find you another who will not agree with him.
—Michel Eyquem de Montaigne (1533–92)

Chapter objectives
- **Describe the relationship between medicine and the media**
- **Give examples of professional codes of conduct issued by journalist organizations**
- **Suggest ways to translate such guidelines into critical medical reporting, by asking whether or not health claims seem credible and whether or not they are supported by strong scientific evidence**
- **Explain why systematic reviews may offer useful information**
- **Discuss the risk of self-deception in reporting**

Members of the medical community often claim that the public is poorly served by the media's coverage of health issues. Scientists and physicians complain that journalists are careless in their reporting, unduly subject to competitive pressures, and ignorant of the scientific process.[84]

Journalists and news editors, on the other hand, accuse the medical community of limiting access to information and erecting barriers to the public dissemination of medical research. One of the barriers that has been criticized by some reporters is the so-called Ingelfinger Rule, which states that a scientific journal will not publish information that has appeared elsewhere. This policy has been adopted by several major medical journals. As a result, many scientists are loath to speak publicly about their work for fear of jeopardizing their chances of publication.[56] The public must wait to hear research results until journals review and publish them, a process that can take many months. These restrictions have generated controversy in medical journalism. Critics say that the Ingelfinger Rule restricts the free flow of information, whereas proponents claim that information released from a paper early on may be inaccurate because the paper has not gone through peer review.[174]

While both sides tend to blame each other for the sorry state of health news, they seem to agree that the quality of medical reporting would improve if they changed their ways.[175–76] Many journalists and editors recognize their own shortcomings in dealing with scientific issues,[175] admitting that they all too often fail to openly question statements by interviewees,[128] rely too heavily on a limited number of sources,[177] exaggerate the importance of new discoveries,[81,138] provide inadequate information on side effects of pharmaceuticals,[178] and misinterpret basic statistical concepts in the health field.[129] Some self-criticism has arisen within the medical and scientific professions as well. Some medical experts have criticized their colleagues for failing to publicly disclose conflicts of interest;[179–80,58–60] distributing inaccurate, incomplete, misleading, or even deceptive press releases and press kits;[181] and publicly promoting preliminary data.[182]

Some scientific works fuel such criticism. For example, a study published by the New England Journal of Medicine,[261] analyzing U.S. news coverage of three popular medications, confirms that media coverage of new drugs often exaggerates their benefits, downplays their risks, and fails to disclose the financial links between many experts and drug companies. Existing financial ties between experts or studies and a drug manufacturer, ties that had been disclosed in the scientific literature, were published in only thirty-three (39 percent) of the eighty-five news stories.

More than three decades ago, Henry W. Pierce of the *Pittsburgh Post-Gazette* claimed that many science journalists had been "suckered into an uncritical acceptance of anything we are told by our authorities—our authorities being doctors and scientists."[183] Pierce said that political writers, police reporters, and financial editors all turned a healthy skepticism toward most of their news sources but added: "But we, bless us, go in with our bright baby-blue eyes all aglitter, our pink little tongues dripping with eagerness, and, pencils poised, faithfully record anything our scientist-gods tell us. Never does it occur to us that these guys, too, may have motives that are less than noble."

Being "critical" as a journalist is generally considered desirable. But what do journalists mean by "critical"? There are different interpretations. Journalists' varying views of critical news reporting's attributes have been described by Ekström and Nohrstedt:[14]

- Emphasizing journalistic integrity (vis-à-vis sources)
- Questioning sources' statements
- Focusing attention on a particular topic over a longer period of time
- Giving priority to news that implies a critique of established structures
- Refuting, pitting different views against each other
- Checking facts undercover (without revealing journalistic mission)
- Using challenging, confrontational rhetoric
- Employing investigational research and analysis
- Engaging in self-criticism, self-observation, and/or institutionalized debates about reporting

Several of these interpretations overlap and can be used simultaneously. A critical approach can be used in prioritizing, planning, collecting, and reporting all news, not just in explicitly investigative journalism. The extent of critical news reporting in medicine is hard to estimate, but critics say it is far too uncommon.

THE REPORTER–SOURCE RELATIONSHIP

The relationship between journalists and their sources has traditionally been closer in medical reporting than in many other fields.[16] Reporters have relied on scientific institutions, clinicians, and researchers to feed them good stories and explain the meaning of their work. For example, reliance on press releases has not been considered a problem as long as the material comes from respected sources. Medical experts, on their part, have relied on reporters to give them the visibility and public acknowledgment they need to enhance their funding prospects.

At times, the relationship can work the other way around. Sources' experience with critical reporters can make them toe the line in their relations with the media at large. According to Avice Meehan, vice president of public affairs at Memorial Sloan-Kettering Cancer Center, the best medical journalists prevent public-affairs departments from overselling their messages.[76] Inexperienced reporters do not. Meehan admits: "We are very aware that the best reporters will be very critical of overstatements and might even build their stories around false promises in press releases, taking institutions to task. We keep in mind that experienced medical journalists will correct us if we take things too far, overselling scientific advances." However, she adds, most medical reporting is not that critical. Public-affairs officers need to be very precise if they want to avoid misunderstandings. If they choose not to make such efforts, hype is not far away. Meehan explains: "Medicine has become a hot topic. The great media interest has moved medical reporting out of a rarified group of writers into a broader band of journalists. Journalists today are less scientifically literate than a few years ago. Today, we are more likely to be communicating with general reporters than with specialists. Some of them are not highly trained."

The cozy relationship between medical reporters and their sources has been criticized by investigative journalists, who suggest that independent journalism implies a more critical approach. Instead of indiscriminately reporting what experts say, acting more as stenographers than as journalists, reporters must check things out and "know enough about the field to smell a rat when there is one." John Crewdson is a Pulitzer Prize–winning investigative reporter for the *Chicago Tribune,* renowned for disputing Robert Gallo's claim to have discovered the AIDS virus and for uncovering fraud in a major breast cancer study. Crewdson has attributed the lack of critical reporting in part to science journalists' blind admiration for science:

> When Professor Schmidtlapp says he's discovered something big, the science writers,
> their collective belief reaffirmed (and their own stature enhanced), don't draw their

guns and make him put his cards on the table. They don't flyspeck his raw data, don't check his funding sources, don't scrutinize his previous articles for mistakes. They don't interview his enemies or call his lab technicians at home for an off-the-record assessment of the great man's work. They like science, they probably admire Schmidt-lapp and they're excited by the prospect that he's right.[184]

Investigative journalists say that, despite the aura of mystique surrounding science, it does not take a scholar to question medical findings and ask relevant questions. It takes the guts to bring sophisticated scientists down to basic issues, an elementary knowledge of pitfalls in medical science, and, above all, some common sense and an interest in the implications of scientific findings for people's health problems. Knowl-edge of medicine, medical jargon, and names of drugs is perhaps less important than one might assume. Andrew Skolnick, a medical reporter who served as associate news editor for the *Journal of the American Medical Association* for nearly a decade, says:

> The first guidance to critical medical reporting is the old journalist's saying: "If your mother says she loves you, check it out!" Even when I think I understand things, even when I believe what I am told is true, and even when I am dealing with reliable sources that I am used to, I try to put their information through a filter, asking: "Do they have a reason to exaggerate, misconstrue, or even lie? Is this information consistent with the other facts I know?" My second guiding principle is: "Unusual claims require unusual amounts of evidence." If someone claims they have a cure for a serious disease, I am more skeptical than if they say one pill tastes better than the other. The more serious a claim, the more critical I get.[67]

Rebecca Perl, science/medical journalist for National Public Radio and winner of the Peabody Award in 1995 for her investigative series on the tobacco industry, says:

> To me, investigative reporting is about trying to right wrongs, to expose problems and injustices. That's really what got me into journalism in the first place. It's what moti-vates me. I tend to take a skeptical approach towards industry and to "follow the buck" in my stories, because in my opinion, they have an upper hand on the consumer. There are powerful industries out there who will sometimes try to stop me: tobacco, pharmaceutical, medical devices, food, alternative medicine, insurance. They might threaten to sue or try to make trouble with my bosses. Business and economics have become such a huge part of medicine and health care in general, so there's a lot to look into. I definitely have a consumer-advocate slant—asking questions like: "This new pill, or this new operation, is it really useful to patients?" or "Why don't raped women get a physical exam paid for by their insurance?"[68]

According to Dan Rutz, managing editor/correspondent for *News from Medicine* on Cable News Network (CNN), taking a critical approach is not as hard as it may seem. Depth of general knowledge and a capacity to reason independently, to think beyond the technical aspects of a medical development, to listen, to contemplate, and to ask are paramount. "I think sometimes we spend so much time asking the *whats* and the *hows* and throwing in the *gee whizzes,* that not enough *whys* are asked," Rutz says.[16]

Some journalists think that a critical approach in medical reporting is very much in line with the scientific approach. In his book *The New Precision Journalism,* Philip Meyer suggests that journalists and scientists share some characteristics in their professional approach. Among these are skepticism ("neither journalists nor scientists are content to rest with what popular opinion or authority claims is true"), openness (both professions document their investigations in ways that allow others to replicate them), operationalization (both search for "observable and testable pieces"), and a sense of the tentativeness of truth (recognizing that today's truths may be replaced by "stronger truths" in the future).[114]

JOURNALISTIC STANDARDS

Excellence in journalism seems to be closely related to professional rules of right and wrong. According to Klaidman and Beauchamp, professional standards like fairness

"What have you done to him?"
"He had the nerve to offer me a free nose job for a page one story on his clinic."

and accuracy are in fact moral dimensions of journalistic competence. They argue, for example, that "while the use of reliable sources may be a part of general journalistic competence, the question of *how many* reliable sources to use when reporting an item that has serious social implications is also a question about moral responsibility."[185]

Medical reporters and editors—like researchers, clinicians, and administrators—may experience conflicts of interest. A conflict of interest is any financial or other interest that conflicts with the journalistic mission. It may lead to undue emphasis or suppression of certain facts. A conflict of interest may arise from a financial interest in a health product company (e.g., owning stock or being a paid consultant) or from some other personal tie to the use of a particular health intervention. It is difficult to prove that a journalist's conflict of interest has actually influenced his or her reporting, but the mere suspicion of such an influence weakens the reporter's credibility. Therefore, journalists should always avoid conflicts of interest that might affect their ability to report a story fairly. Medical reporters and editors should be formally requested to document any potential conflicts of interest.

It is a generally accepted norm that journalists should not accept gifts from their sources since this can threaten their journalistic integrity and independence. But "gifts" can take many forms. "I know that some freelance writers—I won't call them journalists—have special 'placement' arrangements with drug companies," says Serena Stockwell, editor in chief of Targeted Periodicals at Lippincott Williams, and Wilkins Healthcare. "The writer gets a list of periodicals in which the drug company wants an article placed. If [this arrangement] succeeds, the writer gets perhaps four times the normal fee for an article." Stockwell does not want third parties involved when she buys an article, because it is a threat to journalistic accuracy. "I detest placement arrangements. That's why I will only accept contributions from freelancers I know well—I won't risk our reputation."[186]

From this perspective, ethical issues are key to journalistic excellence in general and to quality medical reporting in particular. Thus, journalistic competence includes not only the abilities to recognize a story, to gather information quickly, to use language effectively, and to limit stories appropriately in time or space. A range of additional criteria have been used to describe good journalism, including fairness, truthfulness, significance, independence, and scrutiny. Professional codes and guidelines have been issued to this end.

For example, the Society of Professional Journalists' Code of Ethics states that journalists should "seek truth and report it." In doing so, they should "test the accuracy of information from all sources and exercise care to avoid inadvertent error."[187]

The Swedish Cooperation Council of the Press states in its Code of Ethics for the Press, Radio, and Television that journalists must "provide accurate news," since "the role played by the mass media in society and the confidence of the general public in these media call for accurate and objective news reports." Furthermore, journalists are urged: "Be critical of news sources. Check facts as carefully as possible in the light of the circumstances even if they have been published earlier. Allow the reader/

listener/viewer the possibility of distinguishing between statements of fact and comments."[187]

The International Federation of Journalists, in its Declaration of Principles on the Conduct of Journalists (adopted by the Second World Congress of the International Federation of Journalists at Bordeaux on April 25–28, 1954, and amended by the Eighteenth IFJ World Congress in Helsingør on June 2–6, 1986), declares: "Respect for truth and for the right of the public to truth is the first duty of the journalist. . . . The journalist shall report only in accordance with facts of which he/she knows the origin. The journalist shall not suppress essential information."[187]

The British National Union of Journalists states in its Code of Conduct: "A journalist shall strive to ensure that the information he/she disseminates is fair and accurate, avoid the expression of comment and conjecture as established fact and falsification by distortion, selection or misrepresentation."[187]

The Australian Journalists Association's Code of Ethics states that the members "shall report and interpret the news with scrupulous honesty by striving to disclose all essential facts and by not suppressing relevant, available facts or distorting by wrong or improper emphasis."[187]

The American Society of Newspaper Editors states: "The primary purpose of gathering and distributing news and opinion is to serve the general welfare by informing the people and enabling them to make judgments on the issues of the time. . . . The American press was made free not just to inform or just to serve as a forum for debate but also to bring an independent scrutiny to bear on the forces of power in the society, including the conduct of official power at all levels of government."[187]

Critics of medical and science reporting claim that the stories many journalists write are a poor fit with the high ideals they officially embrace. For example, medical reporting on American television, especially local television, has been heavily criticized for its gullibility. A major objection has been that journalists focus too much on promoting "promising" high technology and proclaiming medical "breakthroughs" without asking for the hard facts to back up these stories, neglecting critical follow-up questions, and merely accepting spoon-fed information as fact.[176]

Gary Schwitzer, former medical news producer/correspondent for CNN, writes:

> Pharmaceutical and medical device manufacturers quickly capitalize on this journalistic naiveté, collecting free publicity through news stories. Physicians and administrators of health care facilities become enamored with their ability to promote themselves or increase their fame or fortune via television. Somewhere in all of this, the viewer (patient or consumer) is forgotten, as he or she tries to make sense of the "new breakthrough" just proclaimed on the evening news.[176]

How can the journalistic ideals expressed in various codes of conduct be translated into the practice of medical reporting?

I'm afraid you're suffering from Reporter's Syndrome, Ms. Walters, and we really do need to remove that malicious tongue.

THE BACKBONE OF CRITICAL MEDICAL REPORTING

As described above, the concept of "critical journalism" has different meanings to different reporters. The following interpretation focuses on four questions: Do the claims seem credible? Are the claims supported by scientific evidence? Is the evidence strong or weak? What is the best way to tell the true story?

Do the claims seem credible?

Many medical journalists say one trick of the trade is being skeptical, not cynical. Tom Friedman of the *New York Times* puts it this way: "Skepticism is about asking questions, being dubious, being wary, not being gullible. Cynicism is about already having the answers—or thinking you do—about a person or an event. The skeptic says, 'I don't think that's true; I'm going to check it out.' The cynic says, 'I know that's not true. It couldn't be. I'm going to slam him.'"[264]

Recognizing false claims. Skeptical reporters do not necessarily avoid reporting tentative medical findings. However, they do not present experts' wishes as if they were facts. It is crucial for medical reporters to doubt, question, and challenge assertions and generally accepted conclusions and to point out the weaknesses and limitations in scientific studies. One of the first lessons to learn is to recognize signs of phony, exaggerated, or unproven claims for health-related products. In June 1999, the U.S. Federal Trade Commission issued a list of warning signals:[188]

- Phrases like "scientific breakthrough," "miraculous cure," "exclusive product," "secret formula," and "ancient ingredient"
- Use of "medicalese," that is, impressive terminology to disguise a lack of good science
- Case histories from "cured" consumers claiming amazing results (their testimonials also imply that their experience is typical for consumers using the product or service; when you see a testimonial, ask for proof of its "typical" nature)
- A laundry list of symptoms the product cures or treats
- The latest trendy ingredient touted in the headlines
- A claim that the product is available from only one source, for a limited time
- Testimonials from "famous" medical experts
- A claim that the government, the medical profession, or research scientists have conspired to suppress the product

Disclosing uncertainties and inconsistencies. Critical medical reporting identifies hypotheses as such, regardless of how compelling they may seem. Hypotheses are not given more credibility than is appropriate considering the amount of empirical support. When sharing speculations with the audience, the reporter makes it perfectly clear that the source has not presented any evidence to support them. Whenever the reporter is covering diagnostic or therapeutic procedures of which the long-term consequences are unknown, this fact is stated. Experts' personal opinions and unsystematic observations are clearly distinguished from scientific findings. Opinions are analyzed with respect to theoretical support, internal consistency, and logic.

Evaluating sources' level of expertise. Having acquired the prerequisite skills and confidence through experience and critical probing, the reporter checks the validity of an expert's claim as thoroughly as possible. Ideally, the reporter will combine systematic reviews of the scientific literature and of large-scale randomized clinical trials with personal contacts with reliable but disinterested field experts to validate expert statements about best treatment. Experts used as sources will have credentials in the specific field the report focuses on and will not be quoted just because they have extreme viewpoints.

Considering potential biases. "A good medical reporter will always be aware of hidden agendas," says Andrew Skolnick. "The best reporters always ask: What's in it for him or her?"[67] All stakeholders have their own axes to grind. The critical reporter therefore recognizes that competition for media coverage can lead to exaggeration or other forms of falsehood in press materials provided by corporate sources, academic institutions, medical journals, professional organizations, and others.[55,181,189] When a source could benefit financially from media attention or is funded or employed by an institution that will benefit, critical medical reporters will disclose this conflict of interest to their audiences, enabling members of the audience to make their own validity judgments.[84]

Being independent.   Being an independent medical reporter also implies independence from colleagues' viewpoints and so-called pack journalism. Independence in this context might mean, for example, having the integrity to refuse to cover an issue that is not worth running, even though other media are covering it. It may also mean being able to judge newsworthiness accurately regardless of which items are pushed in press releases from medical journals and to investigate other areas of research by contacting scientists, scanning specialty journals, and reading more of a scientific journal than the lead article.

Independence may also mean having the persistence to convince editors that ongoing stories should be followed up, covered in features or series of features, or investigated in depth. Moreover, rather than focusing on the issues brought forward by experts in various media outlets, the critical medical reporter will also pay close attention to important issues that are not discussed, including information that is actively suppressed. "It's not what somebody wants to see in print but rather what somebody doesn't want to see in print that really counts," says Ralph King at the *Wall Street Journal*.[53]

Are the claims supported by scientific evidence?

Critical journalists looking at a claim about medical effects should explore six fundamental issues. Investigating issues like these gives clues about whether the claim is likely to be true and whether it is probably significant.[66]

Where is the evidence?   A key journalistic task is to distinguish between opinions and facts. If a source implies that there is scientific evidence for a claim, he or she should be able to provide it. The reporter may ask for a copy of the published article that is said to support the claim or at least a full reference. If no such evidence can be found, the reporter will tell the audience that the claim is based on the opinion of an individual expert and not on scientific evidence.

To whom does it apply?   The medical reporter needs to find out to what patient categories, if any, the results apply and during what time span. Has it really been shown that the results apply to categories other than the one under study (e.g., older/younger, men/women, under different social conditions, for other diagnoses), even after longer follow-up? Or is wider application just a hope? If so, the audience needs to know.

How powerful is the research method?   When a source refers to a scientific study as the basis for a medical claim, critical reporters will check whether the study can actually provide such support, such as determining whether strong or weak research methods were used. In clinical trials, the following general rules often apply: Prospective studies are preferable to retrospective ones; controlled studies are preferable to uncontrolled ones, randomized studies to nonrandomized ones; large studies to small ones, contemporaneous controls to historical ones, and blinded studies to unblinded. A rough hierarchy of methods to study the effectiveness of a treatment is presented in table 6.1.[117]

Table 6.1. Rating a health care intervention study according to methodology, in rough order of most to least rigorous methodology[117]

Large randomized controlled trial
Small randomized controlled trial
Nonrandomized trial with contemporaneous controls
Nonrandomized trial with historical controls
Cohort study
Case control study
Cross-sectional study
Surveillance (e.g., using databases or registers)
Series of consecutive cases
Single case report (anecdote)

How large is the absolute effect? How big a difference does the treatment make in absolute numbers? Compared to what? Sweeping descriptions like "good effect," "high risk," or "effective treatment" are questionable, and the critical reporter wants the absolute numbers.

If a treatment effect is only presented as a relative change—"reduces the risk by 50 percent" or "reduces mortality by 30 percent"—the change in absolute numbers must be checked. This will reveal whether it is an important change or if the risk is so tiny to begin with that cutting it in half makes little difference. Even if the treatment is potentially life-saving, expressing changes only in terms of percentages is not enough unless everyone knows what the baseline is.

How precise is the result? How many people were included in the study? How wide is the margin of error? In pre-election polls, reporters tell the audience things like "party X has 32 percent of the votes, and party Y has 29 percent, but the difference is not statistically significant." This means that party X's lead in the poll could well be due to the play of chance. In other words, the poll would have had to be much larger to ascertain the facts with greater certainty.

The same problem faces virtually all medical reporters, which is why they must pay attention to precision. They should ask questions like "Is the average exactly 32 or is it really 32 ± 7, that is, anything between 25 and 39?" Important results should be accompanied by a confidence interval. That interval is the range of numbers within which the "true" value is expected to lie, with a given degree of certainty (e.g., 95 percent). The more subjects included in the study, the narrower this range will be. The interval has an upper and a lower limit. It is misleading to report only the upper limit or only the lower, as the media sometimes do ("up to 39 percent" or "as low as 25 percent").

Reporters must always question whether a difference between treated patients and controls is statistically significant. How likely is it that the difference is just a fluke? This likelihood is often expressed as a p-value, a number that accompanies a result.

P-values range from zero to one. A *p*-value of less than 0.05 ($p < 0.05$) indicates that, with 95 percent certainty, the result is *not* due to chance. Such a result is often considered statistically significant. If the *p*-value is greater than 0.05, for example, $p < 0.1$, the result is generally not regarded as statistically significant.

It is crucial to remember that even statistically significant results can be completely false if there are serious flaws in the study's design. A statistically significant difference therefore by no means guarantees that there is a real difference between treatment and control: The results may be precise, but they may be precisely wrong.

How well does the evidence match previous findings? Are findings consistent with existing evidence, for instance, from other research groups? Or are they inconsistent? The greater the number of studies that confirm a certain result, the greater the chance that it is true. If a claim is based on a single study, and no other studies have been conducted, there is generally reason to be skeptical and cautious in reporting. There is even more reason to be skeptical if previous, well-designed, and properly conducted studies contradict the new one. The result may be a fluke. Accepting a 95 percent probability that a result is not due to chance (i.e., $p < 0.05$) automatically means that—on average—5 answers out of every 100 research questions are likely to be flukes. A single study rarely offers strong enough evidence to change clinical practice. In some areas, researchers have systematically reviewed all available evidence and combined the results in meta-analyses that, when properly performed, give a more accurate overall picture than simply counting the number of positive and negative studies.

Is the evidence strong or weak?

Below is a list of caveats for scientific shortcomings that medical reporters encounter. They are related to measuring the effects of a treatment called X. This list of "red flags" is not comprehensive, and a study may have severe methodological flaws even if it has none of the problems mentioned here.

Preliminary results. The source cannot present any published scientific evidence to support that X has a certain effect. No results to substantiate the claim have been published by any peer-reviewed journal. The source refers only to his or her own experience, saying things like "I have performed two hundred operations of this kind and I have never seen any problems" or "preliminary results show . . ." or "our results have been submitted for publication . . ."

Caveat: Such arguments cannot replace peer-reviewed, published results. The claims may or may not be true, but they should be treated as unproven.

No control group. The source refers to a published, peer-reviewed study of X that did not use a control group. Conclusions are drawn solely on the basis of subjects' health condition before and after X.

Caveat: Without comparing to contemporary controls, it is rarely possible to determine whether outcomes are due to X, to spontaneous changes over time, or to other factors entirely.

No randomization. The peer-reviewed, published study included a control group, but subjects were not allocated by true randomization. Instead, investigators may have assigned patients to treatment or control according to some other principle, for example, place of residence, zip code, birth date, day of the week, or first letter of family name. Or they simply assigned every second patient to the treatment group.

Caveat: None of these methods is considered acceptable for randomization, because they do not protect against systematic error. There is strong scientific support for using true (often computer-generated) randomization methods. Other methods will give unreliable results.

Few observations. The study was randomized but too small. Investigators did not have sufficient resources to conduct a larger study or could not recruit more patients or were convinced that X would be so effective that even a small study would demonstrate its utility.

Caveat: The smaller the number of observations, the weaker the study. Small studies may generate new hypotheses but are generally inconclusive. It is often (but not always) necessary to collaborate in a multicenter trial to be able to recruit a sufficient number of subjects.

Nonrepresentative sample. The patients included in the trial were atypical in some significant way. Their condition may have been more or less severe than usual ("worst cases" are not uncommon in clinical studies), or they may belong to a subgroup of patients who are more or less responsive to X.

Caveat: If the sample of patients is not representative of the larger population, conclusions will not always hold true for the larger group.

Many dropouts. A large fraction of patients withdrew from X, did not accept being placed in the control group, or did not participate in outcome measurements for other reasons. It is impossible to rule out that they differed systematically from those who remained in the study.

Caveat: If the number of dropouts is not too great, careful follow-up and analysis of these individuals might compensate for this source of bias. The investigators need to ensure that no systematic differences exist between the dropouts and those who completed the whole study. However, if too many subjects withdrew from the study, such compensation is not enough. For example, if 20 percent of the subjects drop out of a clinical trial, its results can be seriously skewed. In surveys, a higher dropout rate is often tolerated, requiring a particularly thorough analysis.

No blinding. Both investigators and subjects in a randomized trial were aware of what kind of treatment they received: real or placebo.

Caveat: Positive or negative expectations may greatly influence the results. Both providers and patients should have been unaware of whom was receiving which treatment, which is called a double-blinded trial. Ideally, those who analyzed the data should also have been kept in the dark as to which subjects got which treatment.

Brief follow-up. The study was large, randomized, controlled, and double-blinded, with few dropouts. Recovery was assumed when patients had been symptom-free for a short period of time, for example, when leaving the hospital.

Caveat: Patients must be monitored just as carefully to ascertain recovery as to establish a diagnosis. Investigators cannot cut corners at the conclusion of a trial. For many diseases, there are established criteria not only for diagnosis but also for recovery.

Irrelevant outcome measures.   In a randomized, controlled, double-blinded trial with few dropouts and a sufficient follow-up period, those who had received X had no signs of disease according to laboratory tests.

Caveat: Surrogate end points do not always reflect true benefits for patients. Mortality, morbidity, and quality of life are generally the most important end points.

What is the best way to tell the true story?

Choosing good examples.   Metaphors are chosen carefully. Potentially value-laden analogies are used in appropriate contexts. Anecdotes are used selectively as a narrative technique and are not confused with scientific evidence. Single cases are not portrayed as evidence of effectiveness. When anecdotes are used to describe common disorders, special efforts are made to pick typical, rather than atypical, cases. When unusual success stories or worst-case scenarios are used, they are identified as such. Animal studies alone are rarely a sufficient basis for conclusions about humans.

Moreover, results from a single study are rarely considered sufficient evidence—however well designed and carefully conducted the study may have been. Inevitable uncertainty is reduced only through repeated research and analysis. The results of an individual study are viewed in the context of previous findings. Do these support the new findings, or not?

Reporting both effects and side effects.   Potential side effects of diagnostic or therapeutic procedures are reported along with benefits.[261] Their magnitude and frequency are noted when known or noted as unknown when that is the case. Beneficial effects and hazards are expressed in both absolute and relative terms, not only as percentages. The number needed to treat (NNT) is used whenever possible. Outcomes given highest priority in medical reporting are those that reflect the needs and interests of the audience. Thus, effects on relevant measures, such as symptoms, quality of life, and life expectancy are preferable to surrogate end points.

Distinguishing between associations and causes.   Risk factors for disease are described as signals rather than causes. Critical reporters not only ask for evidence of the association between a risk factor and a disease but also seek evidence that an intervention against risk factors actually has been shown to benefit patients.

Quantifying and comparing risks.   Media reports on health risks tell who is exposed and try to include the odds for those people. By providing comparisons with other risks, reporters clarify the situation and may help the audience decide how hazardous a particular exposure actually is.

Revisiting topics.   Skeptical journalists are ready to abandon their own cherished hypotheses when there is convincing refuting evidence. This is sometimes difficult. As Philip Meyer notes: "Once you choose a model, you may be stuck with it for a long time. A model that works well enough for the purpose at hand soon becomes comfortable, like an old shoe, and is given up reluctantly."[114]

Controversial issues are followed up whenever possible. If there is too little time or space to cover multiple important and interesting aspects of a major story in a single news report, the thorough journalist will create opportunities to get back to the same issue,[84] perhaps from a different perspective. Ronald Kotulak of the *Chicago Tribune* says that series "are an attempt to correct some of what occurs with a daily news spot story, which is very difficult to handle because you don't necessarily have the time to contact all the people you need to get all the sides of a story."[16]

Giving equal attention to equally substantiated claims. When there is equal support for all claims, opposing views or interpretations are presented in a balanced way. Claims for which experts cannot provide empirical support are presented as less reliable in the story. Special caution is practiced when preliminary results, conference reports, and supplements to scientific journals are quoted. Press releases—whether in video, print, or digital format, and whether from for-profit or nonprofit institutions—are regarded as biased until proven otherwise.

Considering the impact on people's lives. As mentioned previously, the result of clinical trials may be both statistically significant and true and still be of minor or no clinical importance. Moreover, such studies may well omit important aspects. For example, a source who wants to believe that a certain treatment is effective will often focus on short-term benefits rather than on—perhaps long-term—risks of side effects or sacrifices that patients need to make in their daily lives. To evaluate the overall benefit of an intervention, all important consequences must be considered.

It should be noted, for example, that rare but serious side effects are generally not found in randomized controlled trials. It often takes a longer period of actively monitoring large groups of patients who have undergone the medical procedure before one can assume that it does not cause serious side effects.

Claims regarding the costs and cost-effectiveness of a procedure must also be questioned. Which costs have been included, and which excluded? Some studies include only the direct costs for health care and not the cost of sick leave, early retirement, and the resulting fall in productivity.

Science reporter Deborah Blum says: "Medical reporting is really a kind of public-affairs reporting. It is no longer for the science geeks only. It is headline news with a very direct effect on people's lives. With that increased attention comes a greater responsibility. As a responsible reporter, you have to consider the impact your story will have on your audience." Being able to give a story its rightful emphasis, putting it into perspective, without downplaying risks or overstating the hopes, is part of good medical reporting, according to Deborah Blum. "When giving my story a news edge, I must also make sure to qualify that, and put my qualifications pretty high up in the story. Hyping a story so that it gets on the front page might please my editor, but in overstating a story, I am definitely not doing my job very well. The day you quit reacting like your audience, it is time to stop reporting."[36]

FINDING AND USING SYSTEMATIC REVIEWS

The results of systematic reviews can provide journalists and their audiences with key medical information. These reviews summarize large amounts of information, identify gaps in medical research, and label beneficial or harmful interventions.[190] They can help journalists find their way through the medical literature since they also explain how studies on the same question differ.

Efforts to disseminate the results of systematic reviews to the media and to health care consumers and their families include the establishment of the Cochrane Consumer Network.[191] However, medical reporters who are exploring a particular topic and want access to the best available quantitative evidence will have to search actively for it. A useful starting point is the Cochrane Library on the Internet (http://www.update-software.com/cochrane.htm), a regularly updated source of reviews and controlled trials. It consists of four separate databases, one of which is the Cochrane Database of Systematic Reviews (CDSR).

Systematic reviews are often published in medical journals that can be found in bibliographic databases. These include MEDLINE and similar databases. To use MEDLINE efficiently in locating systematic reviews, you need specifically tailored searching strategies.[192]

It is important to remember that systematic reviews, like other forms of research, vary in methodological quality. For example, they vary in how exhaustively the literature was searched, how rigorously studies were selected, assessed, and excluded, and how similar the included study designs were. Complete disclosure of funding sources and awareness of authors' potential conflicts of interest could help users select balanced systematic reviews.[193] For example, some review articles on the health effects of passive smoking sponsored by the tobacco industry have found a lack of adverse health effects, in contrast to the findings of review articles that were not sponsored by the tobacco industry.[190,194]

Researchers are not always confident that reporters are truly interested in high-quality scientific evidence, such as systematic reviews. Many investigators have noted a considerable gap between the scientific and journalistic communities. According to a report entitled *Worlds Apart,* in which more than 1,400 scientists and journalists in the United States were surveyed, 9 out of 10 scientists thought that few members of the news media understand the nature of science and technology, and 3 out of 4 believed the media are more interested in sensationalism than truth.[175]

A survey of 250 randomly selected general practitioners across Canada showed they were concerned about the lack of accuracy in media coverage of health issues.[195] Only one-third considered media reports on medical health information to be highly accurate. Nearly two-thirds said that they rarely read a story that they considered to be balanced or accurately reported. On the issue of how good a job the media do in reporting various aspects of medicine, a rating of good or excellent was given by 32 percent of respondents for the coverage of the results of clinical trials, by 29 percent for coverage of the availability of treatment, by 20 percent for the identification of any risks of a treatment compared with the potential benefits, and by 13 percent for the distinction between various types of research and knowing when to draw conclusions and when to be more cautious. However, more than 80 percent of respondents believed it was possible for the media to improve, with most doctors recommending more training in the basics of medical and health research.

SELF-DECEPTION IN REPORTING

Journalists, like researchers, are expected to be aware of the potential biases of their sources. This is paramount for independent reporting and is taught at virtually every journalism school. However, it is perhaps less obvious that journalists' own cognitive biases might creep into their stories. In their thought-provoking book *How Do Journalists Think?* Holly Stocking of Indiana University and Paget Gross of Columbia University have speculated about how the construction of news could be influenced by journalists' more or less conscious ways of processing the information gathered.[196]

Cognitive scientists have documented that the mind operates actively on external stimuli, so that what people perceive, remember, and make inferences about is not a replica of the outside world but something rather different. Drawing on results from such research, Stocking (professor of journalism and ex-reporter for the *Los Angeles Times,* the *Minneapolis Tribune,* and the Associated Press) and Gross point out that even when people are instructed to be objective, they tend to favor information that supports their initial beliefs. Inferences are often made from small and unreliable samples. Abstract, statistical information tends to be overpowered by case histories or anecdotal information, which is more vulnerable to random variations. People acting under conditions of information overload easily resort to stereotypical thinking. In the context of journalism, the authors speculate that, like the non-media subjects studied in cognitive research, "reporters, even when they believe they are being objective, may seek and select information in ways that confirm their initial beliefs."[196]

They go on to discuss the many tasks in news production from the perspective of cognitive processes. For example, reporters regularly decide which items are newsworthy; categorize people and events and theorize about them; select and question sources; gather, evaluate, and recall information; and integrate their evidence into a final story. Since any cognitive process is shot through with biases, they play a role in every stage of the journalistic enterprise. To take just one cognitive process as an example, categorizing events involves matching new information to a stored category in a seemingly immediate and almost automatic fashion. But this matching is influenced by the reporter's preconceptions, particularly when the new information is ambiguous. The chosen category guides the reporter to theories about the event. Furthermore, it generates a set of questions that are used to investigate those particular theories. When processing the answers to these questions, the reporter is more likely to trust information that is consistent with the theories than contradicting data. Finally, when all the bits of information are linked together, the reporter's cognitive biases contribute to a tendency to perceive relationships where none exist.

Here are some of the psychological biases that could potentially affect medical journalists' interviewing and observation.[197]

1. The eyewitness fallacy. Eyewitness accounts are not always reliable. Prejudice, expectations, the types of symptoms being observed, and stress may cause errors when patients, health professionals, and/or journalists describe the effects of a new treatment that they believe to be effective.

2. Underutilization of statistics. Anecdotes often have a greater impact than statistical information, whether because the information is more vivid or because anecdotes seem more relevant. Some sources, including some health professionals and researchers, are masters of the anecdote. To quote Stocking and Gross: "If reporters fall victim to favoring vivid anecdotal information over pallid but reliable statistics, they, and their audiences in turn, may be misled."[197]

3. Confirmation bias. We all have a tendency to seek, select, and recall data according to our preexisting expectations or theories. We usually test only one theory at a time. If, for example, we are testing a hypothesis about a certain therapy's positive effects, it is unlikely that we will simultaneously explore the opposite possibility, that the treatment does more harm than good. Expectations may not only influence the sources reporters choose to interview, and the types of questions they ask, but also their selection and evaluation of data. As Philip Meyer points out, however, in practice, journalists need hypotheses: "The journalistic ideal is to be open-minded, to enter an investigation with a clean slate, free of any prejudgment. Having a hypothesis seems a lot like being prejudiced. That view, while well-intentioned, is not practical. You can't begin to think about a problem without some kind of theoretical framework. And you will have one, whether you are conscious of it or not."[114]

4. Misperception of risk. The risks that kill or disable the most people are not the same risks that frighten people the most. Dramatic or sensational risks are often overestimated. For example, the risk of homicide, fatal accident, or lethal cancer may be perceived as greater than the risk of diabetes, emphysema, or asthma. In addition, the way in which a risk is presented—how it is framed—influences how serious it is perceived to be. There may be a wide statistical range of risk, even though only the upper end of the range is reported (with an ominous "as many as"). It also makes quite a difference whether the facts are presented as "an 8 percent risk of contracting a disease" or "a 92 percent chance of not contracting a disease."

5. Misinterpretation of regression. If one extreme has been observed in a population, people often falsely predict that other, similarly extreme observations are more likely in the future. However, a statistical phenomenon called *regression toward the mean* implies that extreme observations (e.g., blood pressure measurements) are more likely to be followed by less extreme ones, toward the center of the spectrum.[198] This phenomenon is frequently encountered in clinical practice. However, it is easy for people who are not skilled at statistics to misinterpret it. An example can clarify how this works. Take a group of people with extreme values of a measurement, such as unusu-

ally high blood pressure. The group will tend to have a lower mean blood pressure the next time it is measured, regardless of treatment. Thus, even if they are not treated, the average blood pressure in this extreme group will go down—approaching the mean of the whole population—owing to regression toward the mean. However, since patients with such extreme values of a measurement typically receive some kind of treatment, regression can be confused with the effect of treatment. The change may then be falsely attributed to the treatment when it is simply a statistical phenomenon. The best way to separate a genuine treatment effect from regression toward the mean is to conduct a study using a randomized control group.

6. Illusory correlation. The frequency with which two events are related is sometimes greatly overestimated. People may even impose a relationship where none exists, perceiving two events that occur simultaneously as causally related even when they are not. For example, if a series of complications during childbirth occur in an obstetric clinic that has just introduced a new ultrasonic monitoring system, it may appear as if the new technology causes the complications. However, the cluster of complicated deliveries may be due to chance alone or to some unknown factor. Correlation in time does not imply causal relation. Association is not causation, without further evidence.

7. Fundamental attribution error. We are often more prone to attribute a person's behavior to his or her disposition than to situational factors.[199] In the case of scientific fraud, for example, there is a tendency to explain the incident in terms of a "bad apple" rather than in terms of a "rotten barrel."[1,200]

Medical journalism improves as reporters become aware of cognitive filters and biases and make efforts to evaluate nonsupportive or opposing evidence. This may be a difficult task for time-pressured reporters. Acknowledging that journalistic work involves more than passive, objective reflection of reality, and that complete objectivity is an unattainable, yet worthwhile, goal is the first step.

Other important steps include continual education and participation in open debates about medical reporting. In many countries, science and medical writers have joined professional organizations where they can discuss issues like these. However, two formidable obstacles to an open debate remain. One is fear of reprimands; the other is cliquishness. More experienced medical journalists may have to lead the way in this area. Bob Haiman, news editor and president emeritus of the Poynter Institute, has urged his younger colleagues: "Stop being so afraid, as journalists and news organizations, to critique—fairly but directly—the work of other journalists and news organizations. We have all heard the old saw about the medical profession, that the prime commandment for all doctors is to 'speak no evil of another doctor.' But I think we in the news business may be worse."[201]

TOLERATING AND DESCRIBING UNCERTAINTY

Many important medical questions asked by reporters and the general public cannot be answered in a reliable way. The only truthful answer is simply, "We don't know."

Various circumstances have led to this uncertainty. First, despite the ever-increasing volume of scientific literature, many issues have yet to be investigated. New findings generate new hypotheses, which, in turn, need to be tested. Second, many issues have been studied using inappropriate research methods, yielding nonconclusive data. Third, chance or bias may have produced contradictory results. In all these cases, uncertainty is what medical journalists must report.

Medical reporters and their audiences, as well as scientists and clinicians, have to accept the fact that the health sciences will always be uncertain to some degree. At best, they produce provisional truths that can serve as guidance until more solid evidence is available. Thus, uncertainty and revision of "truth" are not signs of scientific failure but rather hallmarks of all scientific work. Complete certainty can be found in religious beliefs and authoritarian views of the world, but rarely—if ever—in science. Scientists who make absolute statements should therefore trigger reporters' suspicion. They may be drawing more on their own personal views than on their scientific data. Like everybody else, they hold values and opinions that have little to do with science, and these may creep into a statement at a press conference or an interview focused on their research findings.

Scientists may disagree because they have reached different results in their scientific work. However, not even when the data seem unequivocal is there always consensus among medical experts. The same data may be interpreted differently by different experts. For example, they may dispute whether a certain health benefit is worth the costs in terms of side effects or resources. Or they may disagree on whether a certain risk level is tolerable.

Researchers are also more or less prone to extrapolating from data, and some are much more cautious than others. Indeed, some scientists take caution to such an extreme that it resembles nihilism. There are sources who will dismiss even strong scientific findings because the results are less than absolutely certain.[202] Medical reporters may encounter such an attitude in remote corners of academic ivory towers, where researchers are more interested in a good discussion than in a plausible conclusion. But they may also see it among health industry representatives who have a vested interest in casting doubt on scientific findings that show that their products do more harm than good.

Few experts, however, disbelieve their own findings. On the contrary, they tend to believe them wholeheartedly. Once they have committed this act of faith, some also fail to recognize the existence of conflicting evidence. Moreover, as Victor Cohn puts it, "even the best scientists can be gripped by biases, prejudices, political creeds, judgments, based on different training and values, and, at times, their personal economic interests."[203]

Some media debaters have argued that the audience must be more attentive and more skeptical when they interpret news about health.[204-6] Nevertheless, the audience has a right to expect journalists to evaluate their sources. This does not always happen. As veteran science reporter Philip Meyer notes: "Journalists tend to not test reality with their own observations but are content to do their cross-checking by consulting different authorities with different viewpoints. Instead of evaluating the conflicting sources, the reporter may be forced into the traditional objectivist stance which demands the unlikely assumption that all voices have an equal claim to the truth."[114] By contrast, the critical medical reporter won't stop at observations such as "experts disagree." He or she will dig deeper, exploring possible reasons for scientific controversy and following up on the empirical support for different standpoints.

In short, the critical health reporter will tolerate uncertainty and remain skeptical. Victor Cohn notes:

> Scientists who do poor studies or who overstate their results deserve part of the blame. But bad science is no excuse for bad journalism. We reporters tend to rely most on "authorities" who are either most colorfully quotable or quickly quotable, and these authorities often tend to be those who get most carried away or who have the biggest axes to grind. . . . Without being cynical and believing nothing—an automatic disqualification for any journalist—a reporter should be equally skeptical and greet every claim by saying "show me."[203]

CHAPTER 7

Some Challenging Topics

The very first law in advertising is to avoid the concrete promise and cultivate the delightfully vague.

—Bill Cosby

Chapter objective
- **Suggest topics and issues to be investigated by medical reporters**

INVESTIGATING PROMOTION OF HEALTH AND MEDICAL PRODUCTS

The advertising of health/medical products and procedures offers prime examples of misleading information—and sometimes outright deception or fraud. Companies may try to stretch the indications of their products, for example. Or they may downplay the appropriate precautions, counterindications, and adverse effects, or present them in a way that is irrelevant or unclear. Although there is legislation limiting misleading, deceptive, or fraudulent health/medical advertising, a minority of companies will cross the line.

I heard your recommendation, Doc. Now give me your second opinion!

Historically, most promotion of prescription drugs and advanced medical devices has been aimed at physicians. Traditional methods of reaching them have included advertising (in journals or other media and by direct mailings), personal selling (by sales representatives who make office calls), sales promotion (including such activities as contests and handing out gifts and samples), and public-relations efforts (sponsored symposia or post-marketing surveys).

In recent years, however, advertising has been increasingly aimed at consumers. For example, in the United States, newspapers, magazines, and television programs now include ads for prescription drugs. Most countries and regions, such as the European Union, have banned advertising of prescription drugs to the general public,[207] but companies are finding ways to bypass such prohibitions.[208] The increase of direct-to-consumer advertising (DTCA) of health and medical products[207] is likely to affect what an audience wants from medical news reporting. In 1998, pharmaceutical companies spent more than $1.32 billion on DTCA in the United States alone, 23 percent more than in the previous year.[209]

The pros and cons of this trend arouse debate. Not surprisingly, industry representatives emphasize potential benefits of DTCA. For example, Pharmaceutical Research and Manufacturers of America (PhRMA), the umbrella organization of the U.S. pharmaceutical industry, claims DTCA "prompts people to seek medical attention, promotes informed discussion with medical professionals, and further enhances the dialogue between physicians and their patients." PhRMA also believes DTCA will "raise awareness of conditions and diseases that often go undiagnosed and untreated," for example, diabetes, depression, and elevated blood pressure.[210]

Meanwhile, many consumer advocacy groups oppose DTCA. In the United States, the Public Citizen's Health Research Group argues that "drug advertising both to health professionals and directly to consumers is frequently misleading," that such advertising "serves no purpose other than to sell products," and that there is an "absence of valid evidence showing that present DTC prescription drug ads promote the appropriate selection or the safe and effective use of prescription drugs or improve health outcome."[211] Critics have also expressed fear of overmedication when patients demand a remedy for mild or misinterpreted symptoms. Patients may attempt to self-medicate or demand treatments that are not the best options.

Even if DTCA should prove to increase public awareness of various illnesses and treatments and thus spark useful discussions between health professionals and patients about different treatment options, some ads will be misleading and fail to adequately communicate risk. Advertisers will try to convince consumers that their product is necessary and significantly different from others, even when it is not. The ads may use intangibles, like an evocative image, overstate minor differences between treatments, or present irrelevant effects as major therapeutic advances.

In addition to DTCA in traditional media, the amount of industry-produced health/medical information on the Internet has risen dramatically, reaching consumers and health professionals alike. Some of this information is of high quality; some is not. In any event, Web material is blurring the traditional boundaries of advertising prescription medicines[212-13] and bypassing existing regulations, for instance, a European Council directive from 1992 forbidding DTCA of such drugs.[214]

Other patient-oriented, industry-sponsored activities—some of which are potentially useful to patients, while others are nothing but promotion—include sponsorship of information materials, direct mailings to patients, and disease awareness campaigns.[207] Medical journalists who closely monitor these activities point out that such activities can convey biased messages to patients. For example, commenting on a disease awareness campaign, the *Wall Street Journal* noted that "most consumers have no idea the studies and public service messages actually are part of a plan to sell drugs. The drug companies typically leave few fingerprints, running their disease campaigns through PR [public-relations] firms, patient groups, 'institutes,' and other third parties."[215]

The development of DTCA and of the blurred line between medical information and advertising (e.g., on the Internet) opens new fields for journalistic investigation. Again, the overriding question is: Where is the evidence for the claims made in major marketing campaigns? Medical reporters can help consumers cut through the flood of misinformation if they keep in mind the following ground rules:

- Even in ads, health and safety claims should be backed up by reliable scientific evidence.
- A few studies supporting a claim do not necessarily substantiate it.
- Important benefits do not justify all side effects if they are severe.
- Testimonials of effectiveness are not substantiation.
- Disclaimers may not be sufficient to balance deceptive claims.
- Advertising standards also apply to the Internet.

INVESTIGATING ALTERNATIVE MEDICINE

Alternative medicine is a poorly defined concept that includes hundreds of biochemical, physical, physiotherapeutic, psychological, and philosophical-religious methods. Thus, alternative medicine is often defined in terms of what it is *not*. For example, methods may be called "alternative" or "complementary," if they are not taught at medical schools and if their safety and effectiveness against specific diseases and conditions are not adequately documented. However, even this definition varies among countries. In Sweden, for example, homeopathy is practiced almost exclusively by laymen, while many medical doctors in Great Britain, Germany, and other countries use homeopathic methods.

Alternative medicine raises hopes and sparks hot debates. Critics claim that alternative therapists without medical training contribute to missed or inaccurate diagnoses, ignore counterindications, and delay conventional treatment. Nevertheless, many patients feel that alternative methods might help them. Even in industrialized nations, many turn to alternative methods,[216-17] including severely or chronically ill people who are willing to try every possibility and patients who are disappointed with conventional therapies.

In response to the interest in evaluating the effects of alternative therapies, the Office of Alternative Medicine (OAM) was established in 1992 as a part of the National Institutes of Health (NIH) by a U.S. congressional mandate. OAM's mission is to facilitate the evaluation of alternative medical treatments' effectiveness and to conduct research. In 1998, criticism was raised because, out of the thirty research grants the office awarded in 1993, only nine had resulted in published papers found in the MEDLINE database.[218]

There are important reasons for medical reporters to cover this field and to ask as many critical questions as they would for any other medical story. Here are some issues that reporters should bear in mind while covering alternative therapies.

Many people cannot find a cure, or even temporary relief from their symptoms, from available mainstream treatments that have been rigorously studied and proven safe and effective. There are many reasons. According to some authors, this could be partly "a matter of disillusionment with the often hurried and impersonal care delivered by conventional physicians, as well as the harsh treatments that may be necessary for life-threatening diseases."[218] Moreover, what has been proven effective for most patients with a particular disorder may not be effective for some, due to individual variations. Furthermore, certain patients may have been treated ineptly or may not have gotten adequate help from conventional health care. They may not have been listened to, accurately diagnosed, or offered the best available treatment, or they may have failed to follow the treatment as intended. All such situations should be reported as failures of the conventional health care system.

Most alternative methods—like some therapies used in mainstream medical practice—lack scientific support for their safety and effectiveness. Yet, the prevailing myth is that "natural" ingredients are harmless and that "traditional" is synonymous with "safe." There is reason to challenge this myth. For example, there have been reports of adverse reactions to certain herbal concoctions,[219-22] infections and harm related to acupuncture, allergic reactions after homeopathic treatments, and fractures and stroke after spinal manipulation. Gastrointestinal problems, headaches, and nausea are known side effects of some naturopathic preparations. Overdosing, long-term treatment, and allergic reactions can be harmful. Lacking reliable evidence, therapists have no possibility to weigh the potential benefits of alternative therapies against their potential harm. Claims regarding effectiveness often refer to tradition and unsystematic observations, which may be invalid.

Despite a widespread skepticism toward alternative medicine, partly due to a tendency among some advocates to deny the need for scientific testing, many physicians think it is not unreasonable for patients in the final stages of an incurable disease to try an unproven therapy if they want to. Most doctors who take this approach insist that their patients not abandon scientifically sound therapy (so that complementary therapies do not interfere with conventional methods scientifically proven to have some benefit) and that if the effects of alternative treatment are minimal, almost no side effects should be tolerated (which should be the case for all treatments, conventional and unconventional alike).

The economic incentives to oversell alternative therapies are high. The human costs to individual patients may be high too, if such promotion leads people to delay or reject proven interventions, a choice that may worsen their health. False claims, for example, touting a skin cream that prevents transmission of HIV, can create a false sense of security that leads to increased risk exposure. According to Joel Aronson, director of the Food and Drug Administration's Health Fraud Staff in the agency's Center for Drug Evaluation, "What you see out there is the promotion of products claiming to cure or prevent AIDS, multiple sclerosis, cancer, and a list of other diseases that goes on and on."[223] Less preposterous, but still deceptive, is the marketing of dietary supplements, which are now exempt from FDA regulation. These products flood the U.S. market, subject only to the scruples of their manufacturers. They may contain the substances listed on the label in the amounts claimed, but they need not, and nobody will prevent their sale if they do not.[218] Analyses of ginseng products, for example, showed that the amount of the active ingredient in each pill varied by as much as a factor of 10 among brands that were labeled as containing the same amount.[224] Some brands contained none at all.[225]

In summary, alternative treatments should be subjected to journalistic investigation no less critical and thorough than that for conventional treatments. Here are some questions to bear in mind:

- Is there any valid scientific support for this intervention? If not, why not?
- If it is true that alternative therapists sell hope to their patients, do patients seem to benefit? If there is no scientific support, does it matter to patients that the treatment might be neither safe nor effective?
- How much do patients pay, and how does the price compare to actual outcomes (or lack thereof)? Is there a discrepancy between the promises made in advertising or initial consultations and the treatment actually provided? Considering therapists' ability to keep their promises, is the price too high?
- What is the meaning of promotional buzzwords like "natural," "nontoxic," and "nutritional"?
- What do patients find soothing or attractive about the treatment setting?
- Does the therapy offer more than such "feel good" components as pleasant scents, soothing music, massage, and relaxation?
- Are there supportive interventions that can help patients regain their self-confidence and sense of control?
- Do therapists offer "punishments" or "rewards" for patients who fail or succeed in therapy?
- Have there been any complaints from patients? If so, how were these handled? Are there side effects that are labeled as successes, using such magical lines as "the poison is coming out"?

To critical medical reporters, the crux of the matter is whether an intervention has the effects that its proponents claim it has—no matter whether the intervention is labeled as conventional or unconventional. If no evidence supports the alleged effects, this should be reported.

INVESTIGATING SCIENTIFIC FRAUD

Reporting scientific fraud poses considerable challenge for investigative medical journalists. Whereas *detecting* fraudulent behavior is beyond the means of most medical reporters—because of time, knowledge, and economic constraints—investigating known cases of scientific fraud and bringing them to public attention are important tasks even if such cases are rare.

Nicholas Wade is a science reporter at the *New York Times* and coauthor of a provocative book on scientific fraud, *Betrayers of the Truth*.[200] When the book was published in 1982, it stirred up a lively public debate. "There was great indignation from the scientific community, and it snowballed into a big public issue. There were national committees and congressional hearings on scientific fraud," says Wade.[226] Obviously, he struck a nerve.

In the book, Wade and another science reporter, William Broad, describe in great detail a number of cases that support one of their main contentions: that the fraud detectors and self-correcting mechanisms of the scientific community do not work very well. "Each time a new case of fraud was revealed, the scientific community described it as yet another 'bad apple,' refusing to see the bigger problems—that the supposedly self-correcting system fails and that science is not perfectly objective," Wade comments.[226]

The image of perfect objectivity threatens the truthfulness of science, according to Wade, because blind faith in one's own objectivity paves the way for self-deception: "Self-deception is a problem of pervasive importance in science. The most rigorous training in objective observation is often a feeble defense against the desire to obtain a particular result. Time and again, an experimenter's expectation of what he will see has shaped the data he recorded, to the detriment of the truth."[200]

A similar conclusion is drawn by British freelance writer and editor Lesley Grayson, who has reviewed the literature on scientific deception.[227] While recognizing that very few scientists deliberately set out to deceive on a grand scale, Grayson concludes:

> [I]t may be necessary to admit publicly that the scientific process itself is riddled with opportunities for bias of various kinds which may shade into deception, and certainly make a nonsense of the "objectivity" of scientific knowledge. The scientific community can be rightly proud of the high ethical principles followed by most of its members, but cannot deny that they are as influenced by personal ambition, professional enthusiasms, political leanings and corporate pressures as everyone else.[227]

The following list[228] provides (in descending order of gravity) a smorgasbord of deceptive or fraudulent behaviors among scientists:

- Inventing entire experiments, complete with fictitious results
- Inventing data
- Altering data
- Suppressing inconvenient data, either by omitting specific data points from a graph or report or by failing to report an entire experiment
- Suppressing unwelcome projects, hypotheses, or findings by unwarranted rejection of manuscripts for publication or grant applications
- Designing an experiment so that its results are inevitable and do not test any hypothesis
- Adopting invalid or dubious assumptions that bias experimental results or interpretation; failing to retract publications of work that relied on assumptions now known to be invalid or dubious
- Analyzing experimental results so that they appear to point in a predetermined direction
- Interpreting experimental results in a way that supports a particular theory, without exploring alternative interpretations
- Appropriating for personal gain research data produced by others
- Presenting others' data, analyses, or ideas without credit
- Systematically discriminating against particular individuals and institutions and showing favoritism toward others
- Republishing findings for personal gain without referring to their previous publication

Grayson notes that this list is not comprehensive. Many other inappropriate behaviors have been pointed out, such as publishing multiple versions of the same research paper, naming scientists (e.g., senior scientists) as authors when they have had little or nothing to do with the research, and deliberately injecting bias or delay into the process of reviewing a research publication.

Whistleblowing, as important as it is to the revelation of fraudulent behavior, can be a dangerous and distressing enterprise in medical science. Hence, when fraud does occur and is detected, there is a great risk that witnesses will hold their tongues. Grayson notes: "In a world in which whistleblowing is often regarded as more reprehensible than the conduct it addresses, it takes considerable courage for an insider to take action."[227]

SOME ISSUES TO EXPLORE

Critical reporters who want to cover medicine and health care have a wide range of topics to choose from, since newsworthy health stories abound. There is no reason for them to let public-relations agencies, lobbyists, and interest groups set their agenda. Instead, reporters should independently explore hot issues that are of significant concern to their audience. The following sections provide useful questions to pursue.

Clinical practice

Which treatments are still used in clinical practice though there is solid scientific evidence that they are ineffective or even harmful? How do clinicians explain their reliance on such treatments? If they offer no rational explanation, are they doing anything to move toward more effective methods?

What is the scientific basis for various clinical procedures? How do experts know that they do more good than harm?

Are there geographic variations—nationally, regionally, or locally—regarding the methods used to detect, treat, and prevent various conditions? If so, why?

Have drug representatives, local enthusiasts, or entrepreneurs managed to change the local standard procedures inappropriately?

Have the indications for a certain treatment widened beyond the conditions for which the treatment was originally intended (and for which the effects have been studied)? Is this widening supported by solid scientific evidence? If not, is it at least being systematically evaluated?

Public health policy and health services access and delivery

Are there people entitled to health care services who do not have adequate access? If so, who and why? Who is responsible? Is anything being done about it?

Are certain demonstrably effective diagnostic or treatment methods offered only to some groups and not to others? Why? Who is responsible? Is anything being done about it?

What are the costs (direct and indirect) for treating or not treating a certain condition effectively?

How well do publicly funded health promotion or disease prevention programs actually work? Have scientific evaluations been carried out? If so, are the demonstrated effects proportional to the costs for these programs?

Lifestyle and risk behaviors

How strong is the association between a certain risk factor and a particular disease? Is there any evidence that the risk factor is also the cause, that is, that reducing the risk factor will also reduce the disease burden? How solid is that evidence?

How effective is a large disease prevention program aimed at changing risky behavior? Is it being systematically evaluated, and is there a control group? If not, why not?

What are the costs (direct and indirect) for preventing or not preventing a certain condition?

Do health professionals give patients advice about (or support to change) certain unhealthy habits or risky behaviors? How is that advice (or support) given? Is it likely to make a difference, considering scientific evidence in the field of patient education?

Ethics, conflicts of interest

How well does a certain practice square with generally accepted medical ethical principles, for example, promoting patients' self-determination and autonomy, minimizing suffering, maximizing well-being, maintaining confidentiality, telling the truth, and treating patients equally, without regard to their age, sex, socioeconomic status, race, ethnicity, religion, and sexual preference? Are good intentions more important than good outcomes?

Who are the stakeholders? Does a certain practice mean that some stakeholders win and others lose? What are the possible short-term and long-term consequences of alternative actions?

What ethical principles are supported or threatened in health care at the beginning of life, at the end of life, in everyday situations involving patient choice?

What ethical principles are supported or threatened by advertising, alternative medicine, and such controversial interventions as in vitro fertilization, genetic engineering, euthanasia, abortion, and organ donation and transplantation?

Research funding

What sorts of research topics are funded or not funded by major grant-making institutions?

Who is on the ethics committee of a hospital? What kind of research has been approved or not approved by that hospital?

Are any vested interests involved in funding or approval decisions? If so, in what direction could they skew research policy?

Could sponsors have influenced the way individual research questions were framed, studied, and/or reported?

Do research projects cover the aspects of treatment that are most important to patients? For example, are long-term results included? What about quality of life and side effects that are not dangerous but are bothersome in daily life?

Are potentially important research results systematically underreported because they did not show the desired effect? Or because no difference was found between the experiment group and the control group?

Treatment effects

When people claim that a new method is effective, how do they support that claim? Is it something that they just "know," "have observed," or "found"? Or have the purported effects actually been demonstrated in studies or experiments? If so, where are the data? How solid are they? Have the same results been tested elsewhere, with similar results, making them more reliable?

What claims are made by companies that produce a particular drug or medical device, and how well are these claims substantiated by reliable clinical research on human beings? Did the researchers take into account such variables as age, sex, occupation, income, ethnicity, race, the presence of other diseases and lifestyle risks (e.g., smoking)? Are the measured outcomes relevant to patients, or are surrogate end points used?

CHAPTER 8

Medical Journalism Online

Chapter objectives
- **Describe how reporters can find useful Websites**
- **Categorize search tools on the World Wide Web, and explain the relative strengths and weaknesses of different categories**
- **Discuss the variable accuracy of medical Websites**
- **Give examples of scientific databases related to health and medicine**
- **Explore the potential usefulness of other online sources, including public-relations services, LISTSERVs, news-groups, library catalogs, and electronic medical journals**
- **Give examples of how the Internet is remodeling medical journalism**

The Internet is an increasingly valuable tool for journalists and medium for publishers. Journalists routinely use the World Wide Web to locate sources. They also gather ideas by subscribing to mailing lists (LISTSERVs) and participating in newsgroups, and they use search engines to scan information published on the Web. The Internet offers convenient access to databases containing entries from printed or broadcast news media. There is a wealth of scientific papers, systematic reviews, government records, insurance records, business reports, encyclopedias, graphics, and medical dictionaries to be tapped as well. Finally, electronic publishing on the Net, with its vast reach, poses an exciting challenge for medical reporters.

Some observers argue that patients and other consumers who access medical information on the Internet will increasingly pressure caregivers to use up-to-date evidence and get better acquainted with information technology.[229] Medical journalists might already be experiencing similar pressure. Computer-savvy patients and their families are becoming a more demanding audience. They can easily learn about controversies and conflicting information from sources other than the press. Access to news about clinical research, practice guidelines, and medical products is becoming less exclusive all the time. For many people, traditional journalistic reports may not remain the primary source of medical news, unless journalists provide some added value.

Will there in fact be less need for the traditional journalist in the future, when the public can get information directly from sources and from various information services? Probably not. Quackery, deceptive advertising, and misleading medical anecdotes from the Internet will continue to confuse users who are unable to discriminate between high-quality scientific evidence and rumors, superstition, or lies. Surveys of Internet users suggest that many are concerned about the quality of medical information they get from the Web.[230]

Thus, the need for critical reporting is unlikely to ebb as we move further and further into the Information Age. At the same time, there will likely be less demand for reporters who simply rewrite public-relations material. For consumers who are able to access medical resources and databases on the Internet, tapping the same knowledge base that reporters and health professionals use, the value that future medical reporters can add may increasingly involve quality filtering, critical analysis, and overview. Journalists who have the most ability to search, evaluate, and condense new information, to qualify the news with comments and analyses, and to communicate effectively are the most likely to succeed in this new world.

Using various electronic media for journalistic purposes is sometimes called computer-assisted research and reporting (CARR). Although this term was coined long before the use of the Internet became widespread, access to databases through the Net has become an important tool in CARR.

SEARCHING FOR HEALTH AND MEDICAL INFORMATION ONLINE

Medical information is one of the most commonly retrieved types of information on the Web. In 2000, based on a survey of 2,700 adults, it was suggested that more than half of American Internet users utilized the Web for health care.[263] According to a company-sponsored survey of over 5,000 Web users (mainly Americans), medical information was accessed weekly or daily by 27 percent of female users and by 15 percent of male users during 1998.[231] According to one estimate, there were more than 100,000 medical Websites in 1999.[229]

Despite the plethora of health and medical Websites, many medical reporters find it extremely difficult to find useful, credible, and unbiased information. Websites offering medical information are produced and used by many different sorts of people with many different axes to grind. The list includes health care providers and consumers, professional organizations, consumer organizations and other interest groups, researchers, educational institutions, health insurers, governmental agencies and other health authorities, health organizations, news media, scientific journals, libraries, database hosts and other information services, and pharmaceutical and medical-device companies.

Medical Websites that were popular among users in 1999 include the following:[230]

- PubMed (by the U.S. National Library of Medicine): http://www.ncbi.nlm.nih.gov/PubMed/

- *British Medical Journal* (*BMJ*): http://www.bmj.com
- Medscape: http://www.medscape.com
- Intelihealth (by Aetna U.S. Healthcare and Johns Hopkins University and Health System): http://www.intelihealth.com
- Mayo Clinic Health Oasis: http://www.mayohealth.org
- Centers for Disease Control: http://www.cdc.gov
- *The Lancet:* http://www.thelancet.com
- HealthGate.com (by HealthGate Data Corp): http://www.healthgate.com

Many paths can lead users to a particular Website.[232] Reporters find Websites through such means as the ones listed below:

- suggestions by peers, news media reports, and advertising
- Link lists ("jump sites"), for example, on Medscape (http://www. medscape.com), HealthWeb (http://www.healthweb.org), WebMedLit (http://www.webmedlit.com), Uncle (http://uncle1.med.unc.edu)
- Global search tools, for example, AltaVista (http://www.altavista.com), Infoseek (http://www.infoseek.go.com), HotBot (http://www.hotbot.com), Google (http://www.google.com), Fast Search (http://www.alltheweb.com), Excite (http://www.excite.com), Yahoo (http://www.yahoo.com), Lycos (http:// www.lycos.com), Northern Light (http://www.northernlight.com), Direct Hit (http://www.directhit.com)
- Medical search tools (topic specific), for example, MedHunt (http://www. hon.ch/cgi-bin/find), CliniWeb (http://www.ohsu.edu/cliniweb), MedWeb (http://www.MedWeb.Emory.Edu/MedWeb/), Medical World Search (http:// www.mwsearch.com/selection_of_sites.html), Hardin Meta Directory of Internet Health Resources (http://www.lib.uiowa.edu/hardin/md/index. html), Yahoo Health (http://www.yahoo.com/Health/Medicine), Medical Matrix (http://www.medmatrix.org)
- Regional search tools, for example, UKmax.com, AltaVista Canada, Ananzi (South Africa), Anzwers (Australia and New Zealand)
- Multiple search engines ("metasearchers"), for example, Ixquick (http:// www.ixquick.com), MetaCrawler (http://www.metacrawler.com), Dogpile (http://www.dogpile.com), SearchCaddy (http://www.searchcaddy.com), Search.com (http://www.search.com), AskJeeves (http://www.askjeeves.com), ProFusion (http://www.profusion.com)

Searching the Internet effectively requires practice. Getting familiar with the different strengths and weaknesses of various search services is a first step. The search tools listed above can also be categorized in the following way:[233]

- Free-text search engines (e.g., AltaVista, Northern Light), which interrogate a database of Internet resources

- Subject directories (e.g., Yahoo Health, Librarians' Index to the Internet, The Invisible Web Catalog), which users can browse/search
- Evaluated subject catalogs (e.g., Medical Matrix, OMNI, CliniWeb), which users can browse/search

The main strengths of free-text search engines are that they allow specific search strings and that very few searches fail to provide any hits at all.[233] Among their weaknesses are that indiscriminate retrievals result in many irrelevant hits and that resources included in their databases have not been evaluated in any way.

Subject directories, which are similar to a book's table of contents, do not require that users employ highly specific search terms. One can simply browse one's way down to relevant categories and subcategories in a logical way, which may be an advantage.[233] On the other hand, these directories are generally smaller than the databases of search engines and may leave out important sites.

While most subject directories have not been evaluated for quality, some have been compiled by health librarians and other professionals, using their best judgment to make a crude selection. Such evaluated catalogs often provide brief descriptive entries, which aid users in finding relevant sites.

Using free-text search engines and subject directories is supposedly a self-instructive process. The "help" and "search tips" pages provided at each search engine's Website specify how that particular engine works. For example, users may learn that capitalization of a term narrows the search, and that wildcards (*) can be used to cover in a single search several terms that begin the same way but have different endings. (For instance, the search term *medic** will fetch up medic, medics, medicine, medical, Medicare—but also Medici, Medicean, etc.) Quotation marks can be used for phrases and names in which the terms need to appear together and in the right order, as in *"blood pressure."*

Not all search engines work the same way, but some basic principles apply generally. Database searches and general search engines on the Internet use Boolean logic (named after the British mathematician George Boole). This technique allows users to combine a number of search terms using logical operators. The words OR, AND, and NOT are such operators.

The operator OR finds all items that contain at least one of the specified terms. For example, the search string *blood OR pressure* will search for documents that contain either *blood* or *pressure* or both. In many well-known search engines, such as AltaVista, Excite, Infoseek, and MetaCrawler, OR is used as a preset operator. This means that if the search string reads *blood pressure,* the search will hit documents that contain either *blood* or *pressure* or both anywhere in the text.

AND means that the search will yield a hit if all the terms occur in an item. For example, searching for *blood AND pressure* will only find documents that contain both words somewhere in the text, not necessarily adjacent.

The operator NOT prevents hits on items that include a specified term; that is, it excludes all documents containing that term. The search string *blood NOT pressure* hits documents that contain *blood* but not those containing *pressure.*

A few Internet search engines allow the proximity operator NEAR. It determines that terms must appear close to each other within a document. NEAR works as a restrictive AND. For example, *blood NEAR pressure* hits documents in which both terms appear within a certain distance from each other in the text. Exactly how close they must be to each other depends on the particular search engine. For example, NEAR in AltaVista means no more than ten words apart, but it means twenty-five words apart in Lycos.

In many search engines, symbols can be used to represent Boolean logical operators. The symbol + indicates that a search term is required. The search string *+blood +pressure* is the same as *blood AND pressure*.

The − sign is used to exclude documents that contain a certain term. Searching for *blood −pressure* is the same as searching for *blood NOT pressure*.

Furthermore, search terms combined by logical operators can be grouped using parentheses (or other grouping methods). For example, the search string *hypertension OR (blood AND pressure)* means something quite different from *(hypertension OR blood) AND pressure*. If no grouping is indicated by the user, the same search string might be interpreted differently by different search engines.

Major search engines always offer such advanced search options, allowing users to specify their questions. The difference between an "advanced" and a "simple" query is that the "advanced" one is more precise and explicit. Simple queries may suffice for uncomplicated searches. When several search terms are entered into a simple query, and no logical operators are specified by the user to combine them, the search engine will still translate the query into its own logical search string. But the engine will choose a preset logical operator (a so-called default operator), which may not suit the user's purposes.

Journalists working under time pressure therefore need to decide how specific they want their searches to be. Broad, inclusive searches (e.g., those that combine search terms with the operator OR) will yield many hits. On the one hand, the odds are good that some of them will be relevant. On the other, the relevant hits may be buried in a mass of irrelevant ones. Still, this strategy may be fruitful for users who are not at all familiar with the topic.

Narrowing a query's focus by being more specific (e.g., requiring that all search terms are included in a hit by using the logical operator AND) means lower odds that the search will result in any hits. However, if it does, these hits are more likely to be relevant. The specific approach is particularly effective when the user is already familiar with a topic.

ACCURACY OF HEALTH AND MEDICAL WEBSITES

Reporters who use the Internet to research a story must bring all their critical powers to bear on appraising the information they get. The Web is inclusive enough to host charlatans, quacks, quasi scientists, and frauds, alongside distinguished scientists and experienced clinicians. False claims about treatment effects and disproportionate alarms about health risks are common. Marketing of products is not restricted to clear advertisements but may appear in journalistic or scientific formats. So while the Web offers a wealth of useful medical information, it also has a morass of misinformation and outright falsehoods.

Certain unique features of the Web make the quality of information in this mass medium particularly shaky:[234]

- Unlike traditional media, the Web does not necessarily apply editorial control at the production stage. Just about anyone with basic computer skills can publish, and published information can be modified rapidly. The initial production cost can be low, and the reach can be wide. The information may be true or false, up-to-date or outdated, biased or unbiased, fiction or fact.
- Even accurate information can be misleading because information on the Internet can be retrieved out of context. A trivial fact that is presented without a proper frame of reference, without background, may seem revolutionary. For example, the fact that a particular malignant tumor can be surgically removed may seem persuasive for patients suffering from that disease. However, getting rid of the visible tumor does not automatically help these patients, since the disease may already have spread microscopically to other organs. In such cases, surgical interventions add neither years of life nor quality of life. Simple information about getting rid of the tumor with surgery is therefore incomplete and potentially misleading.
- Unlike printed media, Websites are not always accessed via a "front" page. Information can be accessed directly without entering the site via context pages or "cover" pages containing disclaimers, warnings, and the like. In particular, the line between editorial content and advertisements is often blurred.[229]

Again, the challenge for reporters is to separate the wheat from the chaff. Some gateway sites on the Web make a selection for the users on the basis of more or less reliable quality criteria.[235] Other Web services are dedicated to finding and listing the worst cases of misinformation. For example, American psychiatrist Dr. Stephen Barrett hosts a Website called Quackwatch (http://www.quackwatch.com), which provides a long case list of questionable phenomena on and off the Internet. This site defines quackery as "anything involving overpromotion in the field of health." The extensive lists of quackery published here and elsewhere show that medical reporters must beware.

The questionable accuracy of some information on the Web has been pointed out repeatedly by professional groups,[236] individual authors,[237–39] and organizations such as the U.S. Federal Trade Commission (FTC),[240] and echoed by the news media.[241–43] For example, in a systematic review of Web-based advice on managing fever in children at home, only four Websites out of the forty-one under review offered recommendations that were completely consistent with established guidelines in the medical community.[244] An analysis of Websites with references to Ewing sarcoma, a type of bone cancer, found that some give clearly erroneous, outdated, or misleading information.[245]

One Website that has received harsh criticism in scientific medical journals[246-48] and in news media belongs to "cancer healer" Ryke Geerd Hamer (http://www.geocities.com/HotSprings/3374/index.htm).

Key criteria must be considered when evaluating a medical Website,[249] and efforts to develop such criteria further are under way.[250] Some of the quality issues are obvious to reporters. For example, when inspecting a Website, the user should give particular attention to its owners or sponsors and, in particular, their potential conflicts of interest. Names of the authors and their credentials should be clearly presented, and the user should check for references to sources. Judging other aspects of quality may require special expertise, further research, and consulting databases and other sources.

Reporters should be on their guard if they happen onto a medical Website that displays one or more of the attributes that commonly signal poor quality:

- The aims of the site are unclear.
- The ownership (name, title, credentials, affiliation, e-mail address, and phone number) is unclear, as is funding and potential conflicts of interest.
- The information claimed to be provided is not provided.
- The information is presented in a vague and ambiguous way.
- The information presented is not relevant to the topic.
- There is insufficient evidence that claims are well documented and supported by solid scientific work.
- The magnitudes of treatment effects and health risks are not specified or are expressed only as percentages.
- The probability that the results are due to chance (statistical significance) is not assessed.
- The presence of irrelevant influencing factors (confounders) is not assessed and accounted for.
- There is no discussion of whether the information provided is consistent with other relevant sources.
- Key information is omitted (e.g., not all important risks and benefits are presented, areas of uncertainty are not indicated, other treatment options are not mentioned), and the site makes recommendations that seem unrealistic.
- Sources of information are not listed.
- The site has not been externally reviewed.
- The dates when the information was produced, reported, revised, and posted on the Web are not presented.
- The information is outdated.

SCIENTIFIC DATABASES

It is often easier to find reliable medical information in scientific databases than on individual Websites. Although database producers are often selective about what journals and sources to cover, inclusion in a scientific database is not necessarily a seal of approval.

Full-text scientific articles, abstracts, and bibliographic citations can be found in biomedical databases, many of which are accessible on the Web. Databases containing medical information are produced by libraries, government agencies, health authorities, and professional associations. Some important scientific biomedical databases are listed in table 8.1.

Some useful databases have specialized in systematic reviews of scientific literature. These databases do not simply list individual studies but summarize and evaluate the best investigations, according to predefined quality criteria. Such reviews and assessments can save valuable time for reporters who need to verify a medical claim. The journalist gets access to compilations of studies that have been carefully analyzed by methodological experts and will therefore not have to spend time searching for individual papers of unknown quality. Such databases are found at the NHS Centre for

Table 8.1. Examples of databases of scientific health and medical literature

AIDSLINE   References to documents about AIDS and related subjects. The material is taken not only from MEDLINE but also from other databases and a number of AIDS conferences. Produced by the U.S. National Library of Medicine.

CANCERLIT   References to articles and conference papers from the entire field of oncology from 1963 onward. Produced by the U.S. National Cancer Institute.

CINAHL (Cumulative Index to Nursing and Allied Health Literature)   References related to nursing and allied health, dating back to 1982. Virtually all English-language publications are indexed along with the publications of the American Nurses Association and the National League for Nursing. Books, theses, information materials, audiovisual resources, and conference reports are also included.

CDSR (Cochrane Database of Systematic Reviews)   Systematic reviews of the effects of health care interventions. Produced and maintained by contributors to the Cochrane Collaboration. Reviews mainly of randomized controlled trials. Evidence is included or excluded on the basis of explicit quality criteria to minimize bias. Data are often combined statistically, by meta-analysis, to increase the power of the findings of numerous studies too small to produce reliable results individually.

CCTR (Cochrane Controlled Trials Register)   Controlled trials, including reports published in conference proceedings and in many other sources not currently listed in MEDLINE or other bibliographic databases.

DARE (Database of Abstracts of Reviews of Effectiveness)   Structured abstracts of systematic reviews from around the world, which have been critically appraised according to a set of quality criteria by reviewers at the NHS Centre for Reviews and Dissemination at the University of York, United Kingdom. Different

(continued)

Reviews and Dissemination, University of York, United Kingdom (http://nhscrd. york.ac.uk), and in the Cochrane Library (http://www.update-software.com/ cochrane/cochrane-frame.html).

Although many databases are expensive to use, some can be accessed free of charge through the Internet. One of the most useful gateways for medical reporters is PubMed (http://www.ncbi.nlm.nih.gov/entrez/query.fcgi), the U.S. National Library of Medicine's Web version of the database MEDLINE. In 1999, PubMed gave access to nine million references (in MEDLINE and other databases) and offered links to electronic journals and related databases.

Databases are supposed to be dynamic entities, subject to constant change and updating. In August 1999, the U.S. National Institutes of Health (NIH) announced that PubMed's coverage was going to be expanded in the year 2000. The new site, called PubMed Central, includes "reports that have been screened but not formally peer-reviewed" and material from the life sciences in general, not only from biology and medicine.[251]

Table 8.1. (continued)

health care topics are covered, primarily treatment methods but also organizational interventions.

EMBASE   Articles published from 1974 onward in biomedical and pharmacological journals. Many articles are in languages other than English. About 60 percent of the articles originate outside the United States.

HealthSTAR   Literature of health services research and administration, clinical practice guidelines, and health technology assessments from 1975 onward, 95 percent of which also appears in the MEDLINE database. Included in PubMed.

MEDLINE   References to and abstracts from more than 3,800 journals from 1966 onward. Produced by the U.S. National Library of Medicine. Corresponding printed bibliographies are *Index Medicus, Index to Dental Literature,* and *International Nursing Index.*

NHS ECONOMIC EVALUATION DATABASE   Economic evaluations, identified from major databases and by other methods. Includes cost-benefit analyses, cost-effectiveness analyses, and cost-utility analyses. These economic evaluations are assessed according to methodological criteria and provided with detailed structured abstracts.

PSYCINFO (PSYCLIT)   Literature on psychiatry and psychology published from 1967 onward.

Science Citation Index   References to articles in journals from twenty-five disciplines, dating from 1992 onward. Allows users to search for how many times a particular paper has been cited by other scientific papers. Abstracts of articles are also available.

SCISEARCH   References to articles in 4,500 scientific and technical journals since 1974. Also provides the list of references included in each article.

PUBLIC-RELATIONS SERVICES
ON THE INTERNET

Many corporations, organizations, and research institutions participate in Internet services through which public-relations officials provide reporters with press releases, news bulletins, and in some cases personal contact with experts on a particular topic. Consequently, the material provided is of varying quality, and some of it may be heavily biased. The material is either published on regularly updated Websites, some of which are listed table 8.2, or is delivered by e-mail to the subscribers of a mailing list (LISTSERV).

LISTSERVS AND NEWSGROUPS

LISTSERVs and newsgroups on the Internet offer different ways to communicate with others interested in a particular topic. LISTSERVs are more exclusive, focused, and professionally oriented, requiring that participants sign up. All subscribers receive e-mail copies of all contributions. By contrast, newsgroups are open to anyone, and all postings can be read by anyone who goes to a particular newsgroup area. While LISTSERVs resemble mailing lists (and are sometimes called mailing lists), newsgroups are more similar to public bulletin boards.

In a LISTSERV, a single e-mail address serves as a route to all its members. When any one subscriber sends an e-mail message to that address, everyone on the list gets a copy of that message. LISTSERVs can be either open—that is, anyone who wants to can participate—or closed. Closed LISTSERVs require that subscribers have certain necessary credentials, for instance, membership in a particular organization. Many LISTSERVs are moderated, which means that messages are sent to the list owner before they are distributed to all the subscribers. This is to ensure that all messages are relevant to the discussion of interest.

Newsgroups are always unmoderated, and all messages are posted publicly, available for anyone to read and respond to. As a result, they are often noisy and abusive. Newsgroups are also more transient than LISTSERVs. For journalistic purposes, newsgroups are more suitable for keeping an ear to the ground on a topic or beat.

Catalogs of current LISTSERVs and newsgroups (e.g., http://reference.com, http://www.dejanews.com, http://www.liszt.com, http://www.mailbase.ac.uk/lists.html) are available on the Web.

Table 8.2. Examples of science and medicine media services on the Web in 1999/2000

AlphaGalileo (http://www.alphagalileo.org)   Managed by the British Association for the Advancement of Science in close collaboration with the United Kingdom's Office of Science and Technology, the French government, research councils in the United Kingdom and France, Euroscience, the Wellcome Trust, the Novartis Foundation, and the European Science Foundation.

AScribe (http://www.ascribe-news.com)   Initiated by public-information officers for a group of colleges and universities in the San Francisco Bay Area. Distributes news releases and other public-relations information "from the independent sector."

EurekAlert (http://www.eurekalert.org)   Published by the American Association for the Advancement of Science, sponsored by the Burroughs Wellcome Fund and Monsanto.

ExpertNet (http://www.cvcp.ac.uk/WhatWeDo/ExpertNet/expertnet.html)   An Internet network of university information, press, and public-relations material from universities in the United Kingdom and run by the Committee of Vice Chancellors and Principals.

IDW (http://idw.tu-clausthal.de)   A German science information service that is an initiative of Bayreuth University, Bochum University, and Clausthal Technical University.

MediaResource (http://www.mediaresource.org)   A program of Sigma Xi, the Scientific Research Society, which is an honor society for science and engineering based in North Carolina. The service is sponsored by grants from corporations, including pharmaceutical companies, foundations, and media outlets.

Newswise (http://www.newswise.com)   A privately owned, commercial database of news releases from institutions engaged in scientific, medical, liberal arts, and business research. Contributing institutions pay a fee. Reporters have free access after registration.

ProfNet (http://profnet.com)   A subsidiary of PR Newswire, a company that delivers news releases and information directly from companies, institutions, and agencies.

Quadnet (http://quad-net.com)   Produced by Hall.com Inc., based in the United States. Delivers science, technology, and medical news from universities, research societies, national labs, foundations, and industry.

Vips (http://www.cordis.lu/innovation-smes/vips/en/home.html)   Supported by the European Union, disseminates results of European Community–funded research, from the Fourth and Fifth Framework Programmes.

SEARCHING THE WEB FOR BOOKS ON HEALTH AND MEDICINE

Books can be searched for in library databases and at virtual bookstores. A major U.S. catalog of books, journals, and audiovisuals, called LOCATORplus, is provided on the Web (http://www.nlm.nih.gov/locatorplus/locatorplus.html) by the U.S. National Library of Medicine. These services provide search engines where users can check on a book's title, author, publisher, ISBN, and publication date. A selection of lists of library catalogs is presented in table 8.3. Examples of Internet bookstores are provided in table 8.4.

USING COMMERCIAL DATABASES

With the increasing popularity of using free services on the Web for journalistic research, commercial database producers are fighting hard to maintain their market share. Journalists ask: "Why buy information when we can download it for free from the Web?" Commercial database hosts argue that the services they provide are of higher quality and more comprehensive, covering a greater range of years and scanning many databases in one search, and that their data are more rigorously compiled.

Although the situation is changing, many media organizations still use hosts like Lexis-Nexis, DIALOG, and FT Profile. Reporters use their databases to search for background articles in newspapers and magazines, to see if a topic has been covered by others, and to find experts who have written on a topic, among other things.

Table 8.3. Collections of library catalogs available on the Web

---

Library catalogs worldwide http://www.lights.com/webcats/geographic.html
http://www.library.uq.edu.au/ssah/jeast/
http://www.ub.uu.se/bibkat3/
Catalogs and other book resources worldwide http://www.bookwire.com/index/
Library catalogs in Europe http://renki.helsinki.fi/gabriel/en/opacs.html
British and Irish university research libraries http://copac.ac.uk/copac/
British and Irish library catalogs http://www.niss.ac.uk/lis/obi/obi.html
U.S. Library of Congress gateway http://lcweb.loc.gov/z3950/gateway.html
U.S. National Network of Libraries of Medicine http://www.nnlm.nlm.nih.gov/
U.S. National Library of Medicine's list, including medical research and consumer health libraries http://www.nlm.nih.gov/libraries/
Hardin Meta Directory's list of medical/health sciences libraries http://www.lib.uiowa.edu/hardin-www/hslibs.html
Sweden: Karolinska Institute's list of library-related resources http://www.kib.ki.se/libres/

Table 8.4. Examples of Internet bookstores, 1999/2000

Alphabetstreet	http://www.alphabetstreet.com
Amazon.com	http://www.amazon.co.uk
	http://www.amazon.com
Barnes and Noble	http://www.barnesandnoble.com
BookCloseOuts.com	http://www.bookcloseouts.com
Bookpool	http://www.bookpool.com
Borders	http://www.borders.com
Fatbrain.com	http://www.fatbrain.com
iBS Bookshop	http://www.bookshop.co.uk
Kingbooks.com	http://www.kingbooks.com
Powells	http://www.powells.com

Some commercial database hosts/publishers related to health and medicine are (U.S.) DIALOG (http://openaccess.dialog.com/med/), ISI (http://www.isinet.com/), Silverplatter (http://www.silverplatter.com/hlthsci.htm), and (German) DIMDI (http://www.dimdi.de/homeeng.htm).

When using a commercial database, a reporter needs to know how the search engine works. Otherwise, searches will often take too much time (which is expensive) and be too broad, resulting in overwhelming amounts of information. To minimize costs, some media companies channel commercial-database research through dedicated library staff.

WEBSITES OF MEDICAL JOURNALS

Influential scientific medical journals can be found on the Web. For example, the sites of the *British Medical Journal* (http://www.bmj.com), *Journal of the American Medical Association* (http://jama.ama-assn.org), *Lancet* (http://www.thelancet.com), and *New England Journal of Medicine* (http://www.nejm.org/content/index.asp) offer more or less extensive services. The U.S. bimonthly *ACP Journal Club* (http://www.acponline.org/journals/acpjc/jcmenu.htm) focuses on internal medicine and selects articles from other journals, which it then summarizes and comments on.

The Web has numerous lists of links to other online scientific medical journals. None of these lists is complete, but many are useful as gateways. For example, Stanford University Library hosts an extensive service called HighWire Press (http://www-jbc.stanford.edu/). PubList (http://www.publist.com/) is an Internet-based reference list for print and electronic publications. WebMedLit (http://webmedlit.silverplatter.com/sources.html) publishes a list of links to current issues of medical journals. Medical Matrix (http://www.medmatrix.org) lists links to journals and other online resources in a variety of medical disciplines. In addition, Websites of large medical-journal publishers may provide links to journal contents, although many require subscription.

Medscape (http://www.medscape.com), a multispecialty medical information and education tool for health professionals on the Web, includes a service called Journal Room. Here, users find free access to full-text clinical articles and reviews of the selected articles in some current medical journals. The affiliated CBS HealthWatch (http://HealthWatch.medscape.com) targets the general public.

E-INTERVIEWING

Face-to-face and telephone interviews are key elements in traditional journalism. With the emergence of the Internet, some communication between reporters and their sources is shifting to e-mail (often quicker and more convenient than fax). There are obvious advantages to e-mail communication, including flexibility in time and space. Reporters do not have to request telephone time and set up interviews with busy experts or patients. In many cases, getting through to expert sources is much easier through e-mail than on the phone, where assistants often act as gatekeepers. Moreover, written responses are often more concise and to the point than oral comments.

However, e-interviewing has important limitations. Spontaneity, nonverbal communication, and on-site observations are important dimensions that are lost when conducting interviews via e-mail. Written responses may lack the nuances in tone and inflection that telephone conversations can convey. More importantly, it may be difficult or impossible for investigative reporters to challenge interviewees in writing, particularly if the issues are sensitive and the sources less than candid. Interviewees who feel cornered might go so far as to let colleagues or public-relations officials answer e-mail questions in their place. In such cases, the reporter will probably be unable to verify whether it was the interviewee or someone else who wrote the response.[252]

Finally, e-mail communication is notorious for lack of privacy and confidentiality. An e-mail is about as private as a postcard. It can easily be read, or even altered, by anyone with access to any of the computers along the long route it takes from sender to receiver. Hackers can read and/or forge e-mail and eavesdrop on private communications. As a result, some journalists who deal with particularly sensitive information use encryption programs, such as PGP (Pretty Good Privacy).

PRECISION JOURNALISM

A sophisticated way of using electronic resources for journalistic purposes emerged with "precision journalism." The term was coined in the 1960s by Philip Meyer, who suggested that tools like surveys, polls, and statistical analyses could be used by reporters to bolster traditional reporting methods.[114] Some reporters were quick to see the utility of precision journalism's research methods, which have become more and more popular over the past three decades. Indeed, these methods form the armature on which many a Pulitzer Prize rests.

By using computers to analyze raw data, journalists have been able to spot patterns and trends that would otherwise have remained buried in databases.[253] The journalist becomes more of a researcher, tapping online databases for information that can answer a particular question. This approach means the journalist can reanalyze existing raw data in new ways. The methods of precision journalism have been used to get a local slant on national statistics;[253] for instance, information from large national databases has been analyzed to focus on conditions in a particular city or region.

Spreadsheet techniques—entering and storing data in a "grid" format on a computer system—allow reporters to perform numerical and statistical calculations. Spreadsheets are important tools in precision journalism and CARR. Many online databases and Websites provide data that can be downloaded and imported into spreadsheets or databases.

However, it can be time-consuming to find and compile raw data from databases. The reporter needs to know who collected the data and what the original purpose of data collection was. It takes tenaciousness, statistical skills, and critical analysis to interpret the data carefully and correctly before building a story around them. And yet all this work can come to naught thanks to the fact that databases are subject to error. Typographical errors that result in misspellings or incorrect numbers can lead to false conclusions.[254]

JOURNALISTIC RESEARCH ON THE WEB: SUMMARY POINTS

What follows is a checklist for what reporters should bear in mind when using the Web for journalistic research.

- Evaluating sources is at least as important on the Web as it is anywhere else. Much of the information available on the Web is inaccurate or outdated. Double-checking credentials and identifying information contexts are essential.
- Effective searching includes the use of Boolean logic, topic-specific search engines, and metasearchers. Different search engines cover different parts of the Web.
- Searching for existing overviews and compilations of information—for instance, bibliographies, link lists, and systematic reviews—saves time. Such compilations may be found at Websites hosted by medical libraries and professional organizations, including the Cochrane Collaboration and the NHS Centre for Reviews and Dissemination. Useful sites can be saved as bookmarks.
- Networking with colleagues and sources through LISTSERVs and newsgroups may lead to valuable tip-offs.
- Using information retrieval services, which deliver tailored news items, and subscribing to health/medical e-mail newsletters may be useful. Customizing Web browsers to the health/medical beat can also be worthwhile.

- Joining popular LISTSERVs means getting inundated by e-mail. Reporters who are already swamped by information subscribe to digest versions when possible, and they use filters and/or alternative e-mail accounts to sort the mail.
- Interviewing by e-mail is problematic. Although e-mail is useful for general correspondence with sources, many journalists think that direct contact with the interviewee is too important to be abandoned.

ONLINE PUBLISHING

The Internet is shifting the media landscape under journalists' feet, which is both exciting and challenging. The potential for interactivity creates new ways to communicate. Net communities are emerging. Anyone with a computer and Internet access can publish whatever they want, read what others publish, and communicate in real time with other users.

The Internet is often called a global network, but that is a misnomer considering its geographical distribution. In many countries, very few people have access to computers: I
n 1998, only 0.05 percent of the developing world's population had Internet access.[255] Although the exact usage numbers worldwide are unknown, the best estimate is that more than half of all users are located in North America.[256] Still, even in the developed world, it is not necessarily those who have the most to gain from health information communicated on the Web who have the greatest Internet access.

Nevertheless, the Internet is changing the face of medical journalism, as it revitalizes discussions about the nature and purpose of journalism and the definition of quality in medical reporting. The news is no longer the private preserve of the traditional news media. The fact that organizations that have never been identified with journalism—computer and telecommunication companies, for instance—are entering the field sparks concern about maintaining journalistic quality and ethical standards.

The emergence of online communicators, Web editors, project coordinators, and other media workers raises the question "Who is a journalist?" Some of the new media companies employ Web editors without journalistic training to perform journalistic tasks. Online communicators have a hard time being accepted as journalists. Some even report having been denied equal access to news events[257] or having been left out of union and management negotiations.

Will journalism as we know it survive, when the interactive media, by definition, blur the lines between the receivers and senders of messages? Most observers think that established brand identities of trusted news organizations will survive on the Internet. Audiences will continue to turn to the same news organizations when they need help selecting, organizing, and interpreting news, and the organizations' journalistic standards will be maintained as they compete with a wider variety of other communicators.

Considering how fast the online market is growing, it is not surprising that traditional journalists are pressured to take on multiple roles as their companies adapt their products to the Web. For example, news agencies are developing new formats to disseminate their news to the public. Newspapers develop Web radio, radio companies on the Web expand their services to include visuals, and so on.

Similarly, there are indications that the news production process itself is undergoing change. The evolution of journalism on the Net might entail changes such as the following:

- Deadlines are eliminated because they become continuous.
- Geographical reach becomes global.
- Page space and airtime are no longer limiting factors, whereas users' time and interest still are.
- Interaction with the audience is easier.
- Hypertext is used for a more flexible narrative style, making it possible to provide more background information for those who are interested.
- Undercover research, whether under a different identity or anonymously, is easier to carry out.

All these complex and simultaneous changes will affect the journalistic profession in largely unknown ways. Some argue that if journalists have traditionally acted as gatekeepers, focusing their reporting on the events that they believe are true,[258–59] then the Internet, by which users can access any information that interests them without prior selection, will threaten the traditional journalistic role. On the other hand, others claim that the Internet's unprecedented volume of available information will make journalists' gatekeeping and interpreting function more important than ever. To date, there is little empirical support for either of these speculations, and the issue needs to be studied further.[260]

However, it can be assumed that potentially misleading messages, including public-relations material, infomercials, advertisements, and other biased information disseminated directly from sources, will continue to compete with journalistic reports for Net users' attention. It seems likely that many Net users, like traditional mass-media audiences, will want some kind of assistance making judgments about what they are reading or viewing.[260]

Thus, there will probably be no lack of demand for critical medical journalism on the Internet. Reporters who have the professional skills to judge the truthfulness, significance, and currency of medical news items, who can distinguish facts from fiction and fraud, and who are able to communicate such news in a clear, accurate, and interesting way should be able to find a substantial audience on the Net. Whenever the line between journalism and propaganda is blurred—in cyberspace like everywhere else— such tasks become paramount.

Whatever direction medical journalism takes into the future, it will not be automatic. There are choices to be made. Reporters and editors, field experts, patients, and the public at large can all have a say in shaping the future of medical journalism.

Glossary

Absolute risk reduction (ARR) The difference in a particular risk between two groups: a control group and an experimental (intervention) group. ARR is the difference between the control group's event rate (CER) and the treated group's event rate (EER). ARR = CER − EER. For example, if the risk in the former group is 10.0 percent, and in the latter it is 8.0 percent, ARR is 10.0 − 8.0 = 2.0 percentage units, or 0.02. ARR can be used to calculate the **number needed to treat** (see below).

Abstract A very brief, sometimes structured, summary of the study and its results. It should (but does not always) include what the study tried to show, how the researchers went about it, and what was found. Abstracts can be very misleading, which is important to remember, since they are often the only part of articles that databases show.

Adverse reaction Bad, unpleasant, and/or dangerous effect in response to a treatment.

Alpha and beta errors Alpha errors are "false positives"; that is, the results suggest that a treatment has an effect when in fact it does not. Beta errors are "false negatives"; that is, the results suggest a treatment does not have any effect when it actually does. Large enough samples help avoid these kinds of errors.

Anecdote *See* **case study.**

Association A link, or statistical dependence, between two or more phenomena or variables. A "positive" association means that one variable increases if the other increases. A "negative" association means that an increase in one variable is associated with a decrease in the other. An association may be accidental or may be produced by other circumstances. The presence of an association does not imply a cause-and-effect relationship.

BBS (bulletin board system) A computerized meeting and announcement system where people conduct discussions, upload and download files, and make announcements without being online at the same time. BBSs vary greatly in size.

Beat A reporter's topic area, for example, medicine and health.

Before-and-after study A study design in which a group is studied before and after an intervention. Interpreting the effect of the intervention is often difficult since changes may occur due to factors other than the intervention.

Bias A condition that distorts, or could distort, the results of a study and thus lead to false conclusions. What is observed in the results may not be the effect of the treatment being studied but the effect of bias. Bias may originate, for example, from allocation of patients, analysis, interpretation, publication, and review of data. (This word is also used to describe a personal preference or inclination, especially one that inhibits impartial judgment.)

Blinding Observer(s) and/or subjects are kept ignorant of the group to which the subjects are assigned (treatment or control group) in a clinical trial or other experimental situation. They are unaware of who belongs to which group. Single blinding means that only one party (participants or observers) is unaware. Double blinding means that both parties are unaware. Triple blinding means that even those who are performing statistical analyses and assessing outcomes are unaware. The purpose of blinding is to prevent any expectations of patients, treatment providers, and/or outcome assessors from affecting the outcome of the experiment. Blinding is also called masking.

123

Boolean logic A logical search process commonly used in computer searches, including search engines on the Web and MEDLINE. Connector words, such as AND, OR, and NOT are used to limit the search. These words are called logical operators.

Broadsheet The size of most daily newspapers. Folded in half, the size is called tabloid.

Browser A computer program that allows access to the World Wide Web. Two common browsers are Internet Explorer and Netscape Navigator.

CARR (computer-assisted research and reporting) Comprehensive term for the use of various electronic media for journalistic purposes.

Case control study A retrospective study that identifies patients who have an outcome of interest (cases) and control patients without the same outcome, and which looks back to see if they had the exposure of interest. No intervention is performed.

Case series Report of a small number of individual cases, that is, an uncontrolled observational study.

Case study Report of an observation of a single patient or situation. Also called anecdote, case history, single case report.

Chat group An online meeting place where you can hold discussions in real time with a group of other people. The purpose of chat groups is usually recreational, and they tend to be less informative than mailing lists and newsgroups.

Clinical trial An experiment that tests a drug or other intervention. The term is used for both controlled and uncontrolled trials.

Cochrane Collaboration An international effort to prepare, maintain, and disseminate systematic reviews of studies of the benefits and risks of health care interventions. Researchers, practitioners, and consumers participate. The systematic reviews are published in the Cochrane Database of Systematic Reviews, which is one component of a more extensive electronic publication called the Cochrane Library. Cochrane Centres within the network have logistic responsibilities and help coordinate and support the Collaboration.

Cohort study An observational study of a cohort, that is, a defined group of people. The cohort is followed over time, either prospectively, into the future (concurrent cohort study), or retrospectively, tracking them into the past (historical cohort study). Subgroups of the cohort, for example, those exposed or not exposed to a particular intervention or risk factor, are compared, for example, with regard to health status.

Comorbidity Presence of other disease(s) in a subject, in addition to the condition that is the focus of study.

Comparison group Control group.

Confidence interval (CI) The range of numbers within which the "true" value (e.g., the effect of a treatment) is expected to lie with a given degree of certainty (e.g., 95 percent). The CI stretches between two limits: a lower one and a higher one. A 95 percent CI means that we can be 95 percent confident that the true value lies within these limits. The larger the sample, the narrower the span of the CI. The purpose of calculating a CI is to express the uncertainty related to studying a sample from a larger population, as opposed to the whole population.

Confounding An error that occurs when compared groups are different in some important respect not included in the study. For example, the groups may be exposed to different risk factors other than the factor or treatment being studied. Confounding factors are likely to distort the study's results.

Contamination The treatment assigned to one group is used by some members of the comparison group. The comparison group is unintentionally "contaminated" by the treatment.

Control group The group of people in a controlled trial or a case control study who are used as a standard of comparison. While people in the experimental group of a trial receive the treatment, controls receive no treatment, a placebo treatment, or the standard or conventional treatment. Thus, in a trial, controls represent the status quo, against which the effectiveness of a treatment is tested. In a case control study, the controls are the people who do not have the condition being studied; the "cases" are those who have the condition.

Controlled clinical trial A study that compares one or more intervention groups to one or more control groups. Not all controlled studies are randomized, but all randomized trials are controlled.

Cookie Information sent by a Web server to a browser. Depending on the browser's settings, and the type of cookie, the browser then saves and returns that information to the server whenever additional requests are made to the server. For example, cookies allow servers to customize what is sent back to the user or to keep a log of a particular user's requests. Cookies may contain registration information, shopping information, user preferences, etc. They are usually set to expire after a predetermined period of time.

Cost-benefit analysis An economic evaluation comparing the costs and consequences of two or more alternatives, where all costs and consequences are converted into monetary terms. These attempts to translate both costs and benefits into money are supposed to make it easier to compare different sectors of society.

Cost-effectiveness analysis An economic evaluation comparing the costs and health outcomes of two or more alternatives. Cost-effectiveness analysis is used when the effects of different interventions may vary but are still measurable in identical and natural units. Typically, a relatively simple measure of a health outcome is used (e.g., number of cured patients, number of survivors, or number of life-years saved).

Cost-minimization analysis (or cost analysis) An economic evaluation comparing the costs of two or more alternatives that are assumed to produce identical health outcomes. Thus, it is used when the effects of different interventions are the same. The analysis aims to show which alternative means the lowest cost. Note: even this seemingly simple analysis is usually based on different data sources and a number of assumptions.

Cost-utility analysis An economic evaluation that compares the costs and consequences of two or more alternatives and assesses the value of effects in utilities, units that have been constructed to include not only years of life but also quality of life (e.g., quality-adjusted life-years, QALYs). Costs per unit of utility (e.g., cost per QALY) are compared for different interventions.

Critical appraisal The process of assessing and interpreting evidence by systematically considering its validity, results, and relevance.

Crossover trial A clinical trial in which each group receives all treatments. The subjects begin with a particular treatment/placebo but are deliberately "crossed over" to another treatment/placebo. In crossover trials, each subject acts as his or her own control. The advantage is that the sample size can be smaller. However, this design can only be used when studying diseases that are not cured by treatment. Randomization is used to determine the order in which the treatments are given.

Cross-sectional study A type of observational study showing a "snapshot" of a group of people at one point in time. The subjects are not followed over time. It is difficult to establish cause-and-effect relationships in cross-sectional studies. It is important that the sample of people studied is representative of the larger population, which can only be ensured by random sampling.

Cumulative meta-analysis A meta-analysis in which studies are added one at a time in a specified order (e.g., as every new study is published or in order of descending quality). The results are summarized as each study is added. In a graph of a cumulative meta-analysis, each horizontal line represents the summary of the results as each study has been added (rather than the results of a single study).

Data dredging Twisting and turning the data of a trial, fishing for a significant result (in contrast to designing a study to test a hypothesis). Data dredging may produce "statistically significant" results by chance.

Determinant Any factor that causes a change in a health condition or other characteristic.

Discussion list *See* **LISTSERV.**

Dose-response relationship The relationship between the degree of exposure (e.g., the dose of a drug) and the physiological response to that exposure. Can be positive or negative. However, when it is stated that a dose-response effect was observed, it usually means that increased exposure was associated with an increased effect.

Double blind *See* **blinding.**

Effectiveness The extent to which a specific intervention (e.g., treatment) does what it is intended to do when used in real-life circumstances (as opposed to an artificial or ideal situation).

Efficacy The extent to which an intervention (e.g., treatment) improves the outcome for people when it is used under ideal conditions (e.g., in a perfect trial).

Empirical Based on experience or observation, not on reasoning or theory alone.

End point Outcome. Long-term end points (such as mortality or disability) may be difficult to measure within the time range of a study. Intermediate, or surrogate, end points are sometimes used as substitutes, leading to uncertain conclusions about final end points. *See also* **surrogate end point.**

Epidemiological studies Scientific studies of the causes, distribution, and control of disease in populations, for example, studies that seek to determine the healthiest or least healthy subgroups of a population and to describe common characteristics of these groups. The results of such investigations may suggest relationships (e.g., between certain risk factors and disease), but they do not prove cause and effect.

Epidemiology The branch of medicine that deals with the causes, distribution, and control of disease in different populations.

Evidence-based medicine The process of systematically locating, appraising, and using clinically relevant research findings as the basis for clinical decisions.

External validity Generalizability. The degree to which the results of an observation are transferable and hold true in other settings, that is, to people other than those in the study.

False positive/negative Two kinds of errors, for example, in a diagnostic test or in a study. A false-positive result of a test means that it shows that someone has a condition when in fact he or she does not. A false-negative result occurs when the test does not detect the condition when it is actually present. A study with a false-positive result (also called an alpha error or Type I error) suggests that there is a difference between groups, or that an association exists, when in fact there is none. A false-negative result (beta error or Type II error) occurs when the results of a study show that there is no difference or association when in fact there is. A large enough sample size can help prevent these types of errors.

GA (general assignment) The GA reporter does not have one specific beat but may be asked to write about anything.

Generalizability The degree to which a study's results are applicable or relevant to another group. *See also* **external validity.**

Gold standard A method, test, or procedure that is widely accepted as being the best available.

Gray literature A wide range of types of informational materials, in print and electronic formats, made available by public- and private-sector organizations whose function is not primarily publishing. Gray literature may include reports, brochures, guides, theses, product information, budgetary data, memoranda, and research findings. Gray literature does not always show up in databases.

Health technology assessment (HTA) The systematic evaluation of the properties, effects, and/or other impacts of health care interventions. The primary purpose is to provide objective information to support health care decisions and policymaking at the local, regional, national, and international levels.

Heterogeneity The opposite of homogeneity. The diversity that exists between studies. In systematic reviews, the term refers to variability or differences between study results. Clinical heterogeneity refers to the fact that the results combined in a meta-analysis come from studies that were done on different populations, in different places, at different times, and for different reasons.

Historical control Person or group for whom data were collected earlier than for the group being studied. Because of changes over time in risks, diagnosis, treatments, etc., using historical controls means a large risk of bias due to systematic differences between the compared groups.

Hypothesis An assumption that can be tested with further investigation. To be tested in an appropriate experiment, the hypothesis needs to be specified and clearly articulated.

Incidence The number of new cases of a disease or event in a defined population during a specific period of time.

Infomercial An advertisement that purports to provide the audience with accurate, unbiased information. However, the financial interests of the sponsor are an obvious incentive to present an incomplete or distorted version of medical information.

Intention-to-treat analysis Analyzing the results of a randomized controlled trial according to the intended treatment to which each subject was initially allocated, whether or not he or she actually received it. Dropouts and changes in treatment plans are not allowed to alter the way data are analyzed. Analyzing study outcomes with respect to the initial intention to treat reflects effectiveness better because it mirrors treatment changes and dropouts that are likely to occur in real life.

Internal validity The extent to which a study actually measures what it is supposed to measure.

Intervention An action meant to change the course of events for someone, for example, surgery, a drug, a lab test, a treatment, counseling, patient information, and education.

IRC (Internet Relay Chat). A large, live-chat facility on which anyone can create a "channel." All contributions written by a user of a given IRC channel are viewed by all others. Private channels are used for conference calls.

Lead The beginning of a story. A lead usually consists of one to three paragraphs.

LISTSERV A tool for group communication about a certain topic on the Internet, using ordinary e-mail. Requires subscription, that is, joining as a member by sending an e-mail request to a special subscription address for a particular topic. A single e-mail address (also called the list address) serves as a route to all registered members. When any one subscriber sends an e-mail message to the list address, everyone else on the list gets a copy of that message. Some LISTSERVs are moderated by a human being. LISTSERVs are also called mailing lists or discussion lists.

Mean Average value. The mean is obtained by adding all the measured values and then dividing by the number of measurements.

Median When the measured values are sorted according to increasing numbers, the median is the value that divides the data in two equal halves.

Meta-analysis A statistical technique that integrates the results of several studies into a single estimate, a combined result of different studies. Meta-analysis is a key element of many systematic reviews or overviews and is often used to combine results of randomized controlled trials. It can also be used for studies on risk factors or diagnostic tests. The advantage of combining studies is that it increases the total sample size. Potential problems include heterogeneity of studies ("mixing apples and oranges") and publication bias. The result of a meta-analysis is often presented as a graph depicting the odds ratio (a dot) and the confidence interval (a horizontal line through the dot) from each study.

Methodological quality The extent to which the methods used in a study are likely to have prevented systematic errors (bias). Trials that are more likely to yield truthful results are of better methodological quality.

Morbidity rate The incidence of disease or harm per unit of time (often per year) in a population.

Mortality rate The incidence of deaths per unit of time (often per year) in a population.

Multicenter trials Trials in which several institutions collaborate to recruit and investigate subjects. These collaborations are necessary when many subjects need to be recruited from large populations, for example, from different geographic regions.

Negative study A study that does not show a "statistically significant" result (e.g., that a treatment was significantly better than a comparison treatment). Negative studies are less likely to be published.

Newsgroup Public discussion groups on the Internet (and other networks) open to everyone. Newsgroups take place on Usenet, which is a collection of computers worldwide. Every newsgroup has a name that indicates its topic. Always unmoderated and usually "noisy." Many are archived in searchable databases.

Number needed to treat (NNT) A statistical expression for the impact of a treatment. NNT is the number of patients who need to be treated to obtain the desired treatment effect in one patient. A smaller number means a higher impact. NNT is the inverse of the **absolute risk reduction.** NNT can be calculated when the risks of experiencing an undesired event, with and without the treatment, are known. For a more detailed discussion, see chapter 5.

Observational study A survey or nonexperimental study. This type of study describes what is happening, without any deliberate intervention from the investigators. In a sample of patients, one characteristic (e.g., exposure to treatment) is compared to another (e.g., mortality rate). The risk of selection bias is greater than in experimental studies (randomized controlled trials).

Odds Used the same way as in gambling: Odds could be, for example, 2 to 1, or 80 to 1. Odds are the ratio of the number of people in a group with an event to the number without an event. (Note: it is not the ratio of the number with an event to the whole population.) Thus, if a group of 100 people had an event rate of 0.10, it means that 10 people had the event and 90 did not. The odds would be 10/90, or 0.11, or 1 to 9. This is not the same as the risk, which would be 10/100 = 0.10.

Odds ratio (OR) A way of expressing the effect of a treatment. OR is the odds of an event in the experimental (intervention) group divided by the odds of an event in the control group. An OR greater than 1 (>1) means the treatment is estimated to increase the odds of something; <1, and it decreases the odds. If the OR is exactly 1, then the treatment appears to have no effect on that outcome. However, OR is easily misunderstood (Greenstein J. The heart of the matter: A statistical term leads the media astray. Brill's Content, Oct 1999). It expresses the ratio between two sets of odds.

Peer review A refereeing process to check the quality and importance of research reports. An article submitted for publication in a peer-reviewed medical journal is reviewed by one (or more) other expert(s) in the area. Every reviewer is supposed to check the soundness of a study's methodology and conclusions. The process aims to provide a wider check on the quality and interpretation of a report. It is, however, far from infallible. Many studies of poor quality end up being published anyway, sometimes in less well reputed journals.

PGP (Pretty Good Privacy) An encryption program for sending confidential information (e.g., e-mail or files) over the Internet. PGP scrambles information in a way that is controlled by cryptographic keys. Every PGP user has two keys: one public key and one private. The public key is published and the other one is kept private. Anyone who knows the user's public key can encrypt messages to him or her. But the only way to decrypt that message is to use the corresponding private key, to which only the user has access.

Phase I, II, III, IV trials A series of trials testing drugs. **Phase I** trials are usually performed on healthy volunteers without a comparison group. They assess toxic effects on humans. **Phase II** trials represent the second stage in testing a new drug in humans. They are often performed on healthy volunteers and are sometimes randomized controlled trials. They are supposed to assess therapeutic benefit. **Phase III** studies are full-scale evaluations of treatments. They are usually randomized controlled trials, comparing the new treatment with standard (or placebo) treatment. At this point, a drug can be approved for community use. After the drug has been shown to be reasonably effective, however, it should be compared to standard treatments for the same condition. **Phase IV** trials monitor new treatments in the community. They are usually randomized controlled trials studying long-term safety and effectiveness.

Placebo A fake or inactive treatment, given to people in a control group, so that they do not know whether they are in the experimental or the control group. Thus, placebos are used for blinding. They are meant to be both useless and harmless, that is, without any effect at all. However, there is also a "placebo effect," that is, an effect due to expectations and suggestion.

Population A group from which a sample may be drawn to study.

Power (statistical power) The probability of finding a difference in a research study if such a difference is in fact present. The larger the sample size of a study, the greater its statistical power. The greater the variability of individual measurements, the lower the power. Power should be considered at the onset of a trial, when the appropriate sample size is calculated. A study that finds no significant difference between the treatments of interest may simply be underpowered.

Prevalence rate The total rate of existing cases of a certain health condition in a population at a given point in time, for example, the percentage of people with a particular disease in a country.

Probability The "chance" or "risk" of something happening, calculated on the basis of previous experiences of similar situations.

Prognostic factor Characteristics associated strongly with a condition's future development. Prognostic factors, like risk factors, should not be confused with causes. They are simply indicators.

Prospective A retrospective study examines the outcomes of an intervention in hindsight, using past records. In contrast, a prospective study is designed ahead of time, and people are then recruited and studied according to that plan. Randomized controlled trials are always prospective, whereas case control studies never are. Retrospective studies are generally more limited in the data available for analysis, as the data have rarely been collected with the needs of that particular study in mind. This means that retrospective studies are often less reliable than prospective ones.

Protocol A plan to be followed in a study. It sets out what is going to be tested, why, and how it will be done. Investigators try to adhere to the protocol to maintain uniformity and minimize bias.

Publication bias Studies with more dramatic results and studies that show a treatment is effective are more likely to be published in scientific journals than those with results that either are uncertain or show that a treatment is ineffective. The risk for publication bias should be considered in systematic reviews, since failure to include unpublished studies may overestimate the true effect of an intervention.

P-value Probability value, a value indicating whether or not the results of the study are likely to be a fluke, that is, caused by chance. P-values range from 0.00 to 1.00. A p-value less than 0.05 indicates that, with 95 percent certainty, the result is not due to chance. Such a result is often called "statistically significant." The 0.05 level is equal to odds of 19 to 1 (or a 1 in 20 chance).

Quality-adjusted life-years *See* **cost-utility analysis.**

Random sampling The purpose of recruiting a random sample is to get a representative, unbiased study group. The random sample should not differ systematically from the population from which the sample is drawn.

Randomized controlled trial (RCT) An experiment in which people are randomly allocated to receive, or not to receive, the intervention(s) being studied. The outcomes in the treatment and control groups are compared. The purpose of randomizing allocation to treatment and control groups is that the groups should, as far as possible, be identical at the onset of the trial. There should be no systematic differences between the groups, since such differences may distort the result.

Recall bias Systematic error due to inaccurate or incomplete recall to memory of past events or experiences.

Relative risk reduction (RRR) The reduction of a risk (as a result of an intervention or avoidance of a harmful exposure) expressed as a proportion or percentage of the initial risk. If the reduced risk is 8.0 percent, and the initial risk was 10.0 percent, RRR is $1 - 8.0/10.0 = 1 - 0.8 = 0.2$, or 20 percent. The intervention reduced the risk by 20 percent. RRR alone can be deceptive. Since it is a percentage or percentages, it does not distinguish reductions at microscopic levels from more dramatic reductions. Therefore, RRR should be accompanied by the **number needed to treat,** NNT.

Reliability The results of a test or measure are identical or closely similar when the study is repeated. Also called repeatability.

Resources In health economics, resources include time, staff, buildings, equipment, and capital. Since money is used to trade resources and services, the term *resources* is commonly used as a synonym for *money.*

Retrospective *See* **prospective.**

Risk factor Characteristics associated with an increased probability of developing a condition or disease. Risk factors, like prognostic factors, should not be confused with causes; that is, getting rid of a risk factor does not necessarily prevent disease. Risk factors are simply indicators.

Sample size The total number of subjects studied, called *n* in scientific papers. Sample size is the key to reliability and verifiability. The larger the sample size, the greater confidence one can have in the study's results.

Selection bias In surveys, selection bias means systematic differences between a sample and its source population. The conclusions, then, cannot be generalized to the population. In case control studies, selection bias occurs when only the most exposed cases, not the less exposed, are diagnosed. In controlled clinical trials, selection bias occurs when the treatment group and control group are not equal at the onset of a trial and when subjects drop out or cross over between groups during the course of the study.

Sensitivity (of a diagnostic test) The proportion of truly diseased persons (diagnosed by a gold-standard test) who are also identified by a new diagnostic test.

Significance (statistical) The statistical probability that the result or finding has not happened by chance.

Specificity (of a diagnostic test) The proportion of persons truly unaffected by a disease (according to a gold-standard test) who are also "freed" by the diagnostic test under study.

Stringer A freelancing writer or photographer who makes regular contributions but is not a full-time employee.

Surrogate end point A laboratory finding or physical sign that is assumed—correctly or incorrectly—to predict an outcome that is important for a patient's health and well-being.

Systematic review The process of systematically locating, appraising, and synthesizing evidence from scientific studies to obtain a reliable overview.

Tab Jargon for tabloid. *See* **Broadsheet.**

Validity (of a measurement) The validity of a measurement refers to the degree to which it truly measures the characteristic of interest. Valid measurements must accurately and reliably reflect exactly what they purport to measure. The **external validity** of a study refers to the appropriateness of applying its results to nonstudy patients or populations.

Wildcard A character (e.g., an asterisk) used to "stand in" for uncertain or variable character(s) in a search string in computer searches.

GLOSSARY SOURCES

Cochrane Collaboration's research glossary for consumers, http://www.imbi.uni-freiburg.de/cochrane/cc/cochrane/cngloss.htm

Cohn V. News and numbers: A guide to reporting statistical claims and controversies in health and other fields. Ames: Iowa State University Press, 1996.

Health Technology Assessment on the Net, online resource funded by the British Columbia Health Research Foundation and the University of Victoria School of Health Information Science, http://hta.uvic.ca/glossary.html

Ovid Technologies field guide. Evidence-based medicine reviews—Cochrane Database of Systematic Reviews. Glossary. http://www.ovid.com/dochome/fldguide/glossary.htm

Pereira-Maxwell F. A–Z of medical statistics: A companion for critical appraisal. London: Arnold, 1998.

References

1. NELKIN D. *Selling Science: How the press covers science and technology.* Revised edition. New York: WH Freeman and Co., 1995.
2. GRILLI R, FREEMANTLE N, MINOZZI S, DOMENIGHETTI G, FINER D. Mass media interventions: Effects on health services utilization. *Cochrane Database Syst Rev 2000*; 2:CD000389.
3. CRONHOLM M, SANDELL R. Scientific information: A review of the research. *Journal of Communication* 1981; 31:85–96.
4. MAZUR A. Media coverage and public opinion on scientific controversies. *Journal of Communication* 1981; 31:106–15.
5. BOGDANICH W. Lax laboratories. In Wills KJ (ed). *The Pulitzer Prizes 1988: A legacy of distinguished reporting and unforgettable images from America's best journalists.* New York, NY: Simon and Schuster 1988.
6. BOGDANICH W. False negative: Medical labs, trusted as largely error-free, are far from infallible. *Wall Street Journal*, Feb 2, 1987.
7. JOHNSON T. Shattuck Lecture: Medicine and the media. *New England Journal of Medicine* 1998; 339:87–92.
8. ABBASI K. Di Bella's miracle method. *British Medical Journal* 1998; 316:1617.
9. PASSALACQUA R, CAMPIONE F, CAMINITI C, SALVAGNI S, BARILLI A, BELLA M, ET AL. Patients' opinions, feelings, and attitudes after a campaign to promote the Di Bella therapy. *Lancet* 1999; 353:1310–14.
10. MÜLLNER M. Di Bella's therapy: The last word? The evidence would be stronger if the researchers had randomised their studies [Editorial]. *British Medical Journal* 1999; 318:208–9.
11. ANONYMOUS. More clinical judgment, fewer "clinical" judges [Editorial]. *Lancet* 1998; 351:303.
12. ANONYMOUS. More patients for Italian anticancer. *Scrip* 1998; 2345:3.
13. ITALIAN STUDY GROUP FOR THE DI BELLA MULTITHERAPY TRIALS. Evaluation of an unconventional cancer treatment (the Di Bella multitherapy): Results of phase II trials in Italy. *British Medical Journal* 1999; 318:224–28.
14. EKSTRÖM M, NOHRSTEDT SA. Journalistikens etiska problem. Smedjebacken: Rabén Prisma, 1996.
15. Consumers shouldn't buy into junk science hype [Editorial]. No author listed. Published on June 18, 1999, http://www.drkoop.com/news/editorials/junk_science.html, accessed on Nov 5, 1999.
16. *Medicine and the media: A changing relationship* [Conference Proceedings]. The Cantigny Conference Series. Chicago, IL: Robert R McCormick Tribune Foundation, 1995.
17. *Striking the balance: Audience interests, business pressures, and journalists' views.* Washington, DC: Pew Research Center for the People and the Press, 1999.
18. DUNWOODY S, PETERS HP. Mass media coverage of technological and environmental risks: A survey of research in the United States and Germany. *Public Understanding of Science* 1992; 1:199–230.
19. ALTMAN D, RIDEOUT V. Memo to TV producers: Exercise the power to educate [Editorial]. http://www2.kff.org/content/archive/1358/eroped.html, accessed on Sept 23, 1999.

20. KAISER FAMILY FOUNDATION. Survey Of *ER* Viewers. http://www2.kff.org/content/archive/1358/ers.html, accessed on Sept 23, 1999.
21. BROWN MS. Healthcare information seekers aren't typical Internet users. *Medicine on the Net* 1998; 4:17–18.
22. SHAW DL, VAN NEVEL JP. The informative value of medical science news. *Journalism Quarterly* 1967; 44:548.
23. O'KEEFE MT. The mass media as sources of medical information for doctors. *Journalism Quarterly* 1970; 47:95–100.
24. RELMAN AS. Reporting the aspirin study: The Journal and the media. *New England Journal of Medicine* 1988; 318:918–20.
25. WHAYNE TF. The aspirin-heart study and the Journal's embargo policy. *New England Journal of Medicine* 1988; 318:923.
26. MCQUAIL D. *Mass communication theory: An introduction.* London: Sage, 1994.
27. BLOOM SG. The Legend of the Potholes. *The Pharos,* summer 1996, p. 2.
28. DAVIS RM. Health education on the six o'clock news: Motivating television coverage of news in medicine. *Journal of the American Medical Association* 1988; 262:1036–38.
29. FREIMUTH VS, GREENBERG RH, DEWITT J, ET AL. Covering cancer: Newspapers and the public interest. *Journal of Communications* 1984; 34:62–73.
30. GERBNER G, GROSS L, MORGAN M, ET AL. Health and medicine on television. *New England Journal of Medicine* 1981; 305:901–4.
31. TANKARD JW, RYAN M. News source perceptions of accuracy of science coverage. *Journalism Quarterly* 1974; 51:219–25.
32. WADE S, SCHRAMM W. The mass media as sources of public affairs, science, and health knowledge. *Public Opinion Quarterly* 1969; 33:197–209.
33. WRIGHT WR. Mass media as sources of medical information. *Journal of Communication* 1975; 25:171–73.
34. GRANADOS A, JONSSON E, BANTA HD, ET AL. EURASSESS project subgroup on dissemination and impact. *International Journal of Technology Assessment in Health Care* 1997; 13:220–86.
35. GRILLI R, FREEMANTLE N, MINOZZI S, DOMENIGHETTI G, FINER D. Impact of mass media on the use of health services: A systematic review of the literature. *Epidemiologia e prevenzione* 1998; 22:103–10.
36. DEBORAH BLUM, personal communication, Oct 5, 1999.
37. SHAW DL, VAN NEVEL JP. The informative value of medical science news. *Journalism Quarterly* 1967; 44:548.
38. BURKETT W. *News reporting: Science, medicine, and high technology.* Ames: Iowa State University Press, 1986.
39. WILKIE T. Sources in science: Who can we trust? *Lancet* 1996; 347:1308–11.
40. FRALEY PC. The education and training of science writers. *Journalism Quarterly* 1963; 40:323–28.
41. RYAN M, DUNWOODY SL. Academic and professional training patterns of science writers. *Journalism Quarterly* 1975; 52:239–46.
42. FINER D, TOMSON G, BJORKMAN NM. Ally, advocate, analyst, agenda-setter? Positions and perceptions of Swedish medical journalists. *Patient Education and Counseling* 1997; 30:71–81.
43. NATIONAL ASSOCIATION OF SCIENCE WRITERS. *Communicating science news: A guide for public information officers, scientists, and physicians.* Duke University Medical Center Office of Publications, 1996.
44. ANKNEY RN, MOORE RA, HEILMAN P. Newspaper coverage of medicine: A survey of editors and cardiac surgeons. *AMWA Journal* 2001; 16:23–32.
45. VAN GINNEKEN J. *Understanding global news: A critical introduction.* London: Sage, 1998.

46. GARLAND R. Images of health and medical science conveyed by television. *Journal of the Royal College of General Practitioners* 1984; 34:316–19.
47. KRISTIANSEN CM, HARDING CM. Mobilisation of health behaviour by the press in Britain. *Journalism Quarterly* 1984; 61:364–70, 398.
48. KINSELLA J. *Covering the plague: AIDS and the American media.* New Brunswick, NJ: Rutgers University Press, 1989.
49. GALTUNG J, RUGE MH. Structuring and selecting news. In Cohen S, Young J (eds). *The manufacture of news: Deviance, social problems and the news media.* London: Constable, 1973.
50. GALTUNG J, RUGE MH. The structure of foreign news. *Journal of Peace Research* 1965; 2:64–91.
51. PRAKKE H. *Kommunikation der Gesellschaft: Einführung in die funktionale Publizistik.* Münster: Regensberg, 1968.
52. HADENIUS S, WEIBULL L. Massmedier: *Press, radio and TV i förvandling.* Seventh edition. Falun: Albert Bonniers Förlag, 1999.
53. *Ethical issues in the publication of medical information* [Conference Proceedings]. The Cantigny Conference Series. Chicago, IL: Robert R McCormick Tribune Foundation, 1999.
54. VAN TRIGT AM, DE JONG-VAN DEN BERG LTW, VOOGT LM, WILLEMS J, TROMP TFJ, HAAIJER-RUSKAMP FM. Setting the agenda: Does the medical literature set the agenda for articles about medicine in the newspapers? *Social Science and Medicine* 1995; 41:893–99.
55. VAN TRIGT AM, DE JONG-VAN DEN BERG LTW, HAAIJER-RUSKAMP FM, WILLEMS J, TROMP TFJ. Journalists and their sources of ideas and information on medicines. *Social Science and Medicine* 1994; 38:637–43.
56. RUPPELL SHELL E. The Hippocratic wars. *New York Times Magazine*, June 28, 1998.
57. WEHRWEIN P. Strong medicine. *American Journalism Review*, Apr 1998.
58. RENNIE D, FLANAGIN A. Authorship! Authorship! Guests, ghosts, grafters, and the two-sided coin [Editorial]. *Journal of the American Medical Association* 1994; 271:469–71.
59. BRENNAN TA. Buying editorials. *New England Journal of Medicine* 1994; 331:673–75.
60. GREEN MS. Authorship! Authorship! [Letter]. *Journal of the American Medical Association* 1994; 271:1904.
61. DICKERSIN K, MIN YI. Publication bias: The problem that won't go away. *Annals of the New York Academy of Sciences* 1993; 703:135–46.
62. DICKERSIN K. The existence of publication bias and risk factors for its occurrence. *Journal of the American Medical Association* 1990; 263:1385–89.
63. KOREN G, KLEIN N. Bias against negative studies in newspaper reports of medical research. *Journal of the American Medical Association* 1991; 266:1824–26.
64. DEYO RA, PSATY BM, SIMON G, WAGNER EH, OMENN GS. The messenger under attack: Intimidation of researchers by special interest groups. *New England Journal of Medicine* 1997; 336:1176–80.
65. KING RT JR. How drug firm paid for university study, then undermined it. *Wall Street Journal*, Apr 25, 1996.
66. OXMAN AD, GUYATT GH, COOK DJ, ET AL. An index of scientific quality for health reports in the lay press. *Journal of Clinical Epidemiology* 1993; 46:987–1001.
67. ANDREW SKOLNICK, personal communication, Oct 10, 1999.
68. REBECCA PERL, personal communication, Oct 12, 1999.
69. BLUM D, KNUDSON M (eds). *A field guide for science writers.* New York: Oxford University Press, 1997.
70. ENTWISTLE V. Reporting research in medical journals and newspapers. *British Medical Journal* 1995; 310:920–23.

71. JOHANSEN LW, BJØRNDAHL A, FLOTTORP S, GRØTTING T, OXMAN AD. [An evaluation of health information in newspapers and brochures: What should one believe?]. *Tidsskrift for den norske lægeforening* 1996; 116:260–64.

72. SENARD JM, MONTASTRUC P, HERXHEIMER A. Early warnings about drugs—from the stock market. *Lancet* 1996; 347:987–88.

73. DOROTHY PIROVANO, personal communication, Oct 7, 1999.

74. MARK STUART, personal communication, Sept 28, 1999.

75. LEVI R. Sensationalism vs. journalism [Interview]. *Science and Practice* 1995, no. 2, p. 14.

76. AVICE MEEHAN, personal communication, Sept 29, 1999.

77. NELKIN D. Medicine and the media: An uneasy relationship, the tensions between medicine and the media. *Lancet* 1996; 347:1600–1603.

78. Poynter online: Competence in the newsroom—Narrative and Language [Summary]. http://www.poynter.org/comp/comp_lang.htm

79. Project for Excellence in Journalism and Princeton Survey Research Associates. Framing the news: The triggers, frames, and messages in newspaper coverage. Pilot study presented on Website, http://www.journalism.org/framing.html, accessed on Sept 16, 1999.

80. SBU Conference, Stockholm, Sept 9, 1998: The need for critical reporting. Reported in Levi R. SBU-seminarium: Bättre medicinjournalistik kräver bättre källor. *Vetenskap & praxis* 1998, no. 3–4, p. 8.

81. ANTON T, McCourt R (eds). *The new science journalists.* New York: Ballantine Books, 1995.

82. COWLEY G. Melatonin. *Newsweek*, Aug 7, 1995.

83. LAMBERG L. Melatonin potentially useful but safety, efficacy remain uncertain [News]. *Journal of the American Medical Association* 1996; 276:1011–14.

84. SHUCHMAN M, WILKES MS. Medical scientists and health news reporting: A case of miscommunication [Perspectives]. *Annals of Internal Medicine* 1997; 126:976–82.

85. JOHNSON K. Dimensions of judgement of science news stories. *Journalism Quarterly* 1963; 40:315–22.

86. SCHLESINGER P. *Putting reality together.* Second edition. New York: Methuen and Co Ltd., 1987.

87. DONSBACH W. *Legitimationsprobleme des Journalismus.* Freiburg and Munich: Karl Alber, 1982.

88. ANG I. Desperately seeking the audience. London: Routledge, 1991.

89. COULTER A, ENTWISTLE V, GILBERT D. Sharing decisions with patients: Is the information good enough? *British Medical Journal* 1999; 318:318–22.

90. EIDE M. *Nyhetens intresse: Nyhetsjournalistikk mellom tekst og kontekst.* Oslo: Universitetsforlaget, 1992.

91. EKEKRANTZ J, OLSSON T. *Det redigerade samhället.* Stockholm: Carlsson Bokförlag, 1994.

92. KRIEGHBAUM H. *Science and the mass media.* London: University of London Press, 1968.

93. WARNER KE. Special report: Cigarette advertising and media coverage of smoking and health. *New England Journal of Medicine* 1985; 312:384–88.

94. JACOBSON B, AMOS A. When smoke gets in your eyes: Cigarette advertising policy and coverage of smoking and health in women's magazines. London: BMA Professional Division and the Health Education Council, 1985. P. 36.

95. WALLIN L. Lively discussion between researchers and journalists: Who is responsible for what is correct? [Symposium]. *Scandinavian Journal of Nutrition* 1994; 38:41.

96. BOGDANICH W. *The great white lie: How America's hospitals betray our trust and endanger our lives.* New York, NY: Simon and Schuster, 1991.

97. LEVI R. Läkare som inte törs tvivla och journalister som inte analyserar [Interview]. *Vetenskap & praxis* 1994, no. 2, p. 4.

98. THURÉN T. Problem i den journalistiska etiken. In Carlsson U (ed). *Forskning om journalistik*. Göteborg: Nordicom, 1988.
99. THURÉN T. *Tanken, språket och verkligheten*. Stockholm: Tiger Förlag, 1995.
100. WILTSE DW. Poor reporting of medical studies is dangerous. *Bulletin of the American Society of Newspaper Editors* 1992; 744:28–31.
101. WILKES MS, KRAVITZ RL. Medical researchers and the media: Attitudes toward public dissemination of research. *Journal of the American Medical Association* 1992; 268: 999–1003.
102. KOSHLAND DE JR. Credibility in science and the press [Editorial]. *Science* 1991; 254:629.
103. LEVI R. Vägen till kritisk medicinjournalistik. *Scoop* 2001; no. 1:147–63.
104. KOLATA G. A cautious awe greets drugs that eradicate tumors in mice. *New York Times*, May 3, 1998, p. A1.
105. GORMAN C. The hope and the hype. *Time*, May 18, 1998; 151:40–6.
106. GAWANDE A. Mouse hunt. Forget cancer: Is there a cure for hype? [Comment]. *New Yorker*, May 18, 1998, pp. 5–6.
107. SAYER A. *Method in social science: A realist approach*. London: Routledge, 1992.
108. JOHANSSON I. På andra sidan objektivism och relativism. *Häften för kritiska studier*, 1988; 2:46–56.
109. GUYATT GH, SACKETT DL, SINCLAIR JC, HAYWARD R, COOK DJ, COOK RJ. Users' guides to the medical literature. IX. A method for grading healthcare recommendations. *Journal of the American Medical Association* 1995; 274:1800–1804.
110. ALTMAN DG. The scandal of poor medical research. *British Medical Journal* 1994; 308:283–84.
111. MARGARET WINKER, personal communication, Oct 4, 1999.
112. GREENHALGH T. How to read a paper: Getting your bearings (deciding what the paper is about). *British Medical Journal* 1997; 315:243–46.
113. GREENHALGH T. *How to read a paper: The basics of evidence based medicine*. London: BMJ Publishing Group, 1997.
114. MEYER P. *The new precision journalism*. Bloomington: Indiana University Press, 1989.
115. SACKETT DL. Rules of evidence and clinical recommendations for use of antithrombotic agents. *Archives of Internal Medicine* 1986; 146:464–65.
116. JAESCHKE R, GUYATT GH, SACKETT DL. Users' guides to the medical literature. III. How to use an article about a diagnostic test. A. Are the results of the study valid? *Journal of the American Medical Association* 1994; 271:389–91.
117. GOODMAN C. *Literature searching and evidence interpretation for assessing health care practices*. SBU Report no. 119E. Stockholm: SBU—The Swedish Council on Technology Assessment in Health Care, 1993.
118. COOK DJ, MULROW CD, HAYNES RB. Systematic reviews: Synthesis of best evidence for clinical decisions. *Annals of Internal Medicine* 1997; 126:376–80.
119. ALTMAN DG, BLAND M. Treatment allocation in controlled trials: Why randomise? *British Medical Journal* 1999; 318:1209.
120. CHALMERS TC, CELANO P, SACKS HS, SMITH H. Bias in treatment assignment in controlled clinical trials. *New England Journal of Medicine* 1983; 309:1358–61.
121. PEREIRA-MAXWELL F. *A–Z of medical statistics: A companion for critical appraisal*. London: Arnold, 1998.
122. ALTMAN D. *Practical statistics for medical research*. London: Chapman and Hall, 1991.
123. PETTERSSON E. Fet mat gör dig skärpt. *Expressen*, Aug 30, 1999.
124. GREENHALGH T. How to read a paper: Assessing the methodological quality of published papers. *British Medical Journal* 1997; 315:305–8.

125. STEWART LA, PARMAR MKB. Bias in the analysis and reporting of randomized controlled trials. *International Journal of Technology Assessment in Health Care* 1996; 12:264–75.
126. GREENHALGH T, TAYLOR R. How to read a paper: Papers that go beyond numbers (qualitative research). *British Medical Journal* 1997; 315:740–43.
127. World Bank. *World development report 1993: Investing in health, world development indicators.* Oxford: Oxford University Press, 1993.
128. WILLIS J. *Reporting on risks.* Westport, CT: Praeger, 1997.
129. COHN V. *News and numbers. A guide to reporting statistical claims and controversies in health and other fields.* Ames: Iowa State University Press, 1989.
130. ANTMAN EM, LAU J, KUPELNICK B, MOSTELLER F, CHALMERS TC. A comparison of results of meta-analyses of randomized controlled trials and recommendations of clinical experts: Treatment for myocardial infarction. *Journal of the American Medical Association* 1992; 268:240–48.
131. ANGELL M, KASSIRER JP. Clinical research: What should the public believe? [Editorial]. *New England Journal of Medicine* 1994; 331:189–90.
132. WERKÖ L, HANSSON TH. Skilj mellan experter och proffstyckare [Editorial]. *Vetenskap & praxis* 1998, no. 3–4.
133. ELLIOTT D. Expert for hire. Radio report in NPR's Morning Edition, Dec 29, 1997.
134. NELKIN D. Covering gene therapy. *Quill Magazine,* Sept 1996.
135. WINSTEN JA. Science and the media: The boundaries of truth. *Health Affairs* 1985; 4:5–23.
136. COWLEY G. Melatonin. *Newsweek,* Aug 7, 1995, p. 46.
137. TUREK FW. Melatonin hype hard to swallow. *Nature* 1996; 379:295–96.
138. LIEBERMAN T. Medical reporting. New drugs: A dose of reality. The press too often plays up the positive. *Columbia Journalism Review,* Sept/Oct 1999.
139. LEVI R. Science or propaganda? [Interview]. *Science and Practice* 1995, no. 2.
140. BERO LA, GALBRAITH A, RENNIE D. The publication of sponsored symposiums in medical journals. *New England Journal of Medicine* 1992; 327:1135–40.
141. BERO LA, GLANTZ SA, RENNIE D. Publication bias and public health policy on environmental tobacco smoke. *Journal of the American Medical Association* 1994; 272:133–36.
142. BERO LA, GALBRAITH A, RENNIE D. Sponsored symposia on environmental tobacco smoke. *Journal of the American Medical Association* 1994; 271:612–17.
143. RUDEBECK CE. General practice and a dialogue of clinical practice: On symptoms, symptom presentations, and bodily empathy. *Scandinavian Journal of Primary Health Care* 1992; suppl 1.
144. NAYLOR CD, CHEN E, STRAUSS B. Measured enthusiasm: Does the method of reporting trial results alter perceptions of therapeutic effectiveness? *Annals of Internal Medicine* 1992; 117:916–21.
145. LAUPACIS A, SACKETT DL, ROBERTS RS. Therapeutic priorities of Canadian internists. *Canadian Medical Association Journal* 1990; 142:329–33.
146. JASIEŃSKI M. Wishful thinking and the fallacy of single-subject experimentation. *Scientist* 1996; 10:10.
147. HOOKE R. *How to tell the liars from the statisticians.* New York: Marcel Dekker, 1983.
148. YUSUF S, COLLINS R, PETO R. Why do we need some large, simple randomized trials? *Statistics in Medicine* 1984; 3:409–20.
149. WERKÖ L. Do we know what we are doing? *Journal of Internal Medicine* 1991; 230:1–3.
150. WERKÖ L. Tro, konsensus, vetenskap; vilket underlag krävs för medicinskt handlande? *Läkartidningen* 1991; 88:2129–30.
151. WULFF HR, PEDERSEN SA, ROSENBERG R. The paradigm of medicine. *In Philosophy and medicine,* second edition, pp. 1–12. Oxford: Blackwell Scientific Publications, 1990.

152. Evidence-Based Medicine Working Group. Evidence-based medicine: A new approach to teaching the practice of medicine. *Journal of the American Medical Association* 1992; 268:2420–25.

153. PETO R, COLLINS R, GRAY R. Large-scale randomized evidence: Large, simple trials and overviews of trials. In Warren KS, Mosteller F (eds). Doing more good than harm: The evaluation of health care interventions. *Annals of the New York Academy of Sciences*, 1993; 703:314–40.

154. KOLATA G. Fairness, accuracy, and the tyranny of the anecdote. FACS News Backgrounder. Posted April 1999 to FACSNET, http://www.facsnet.org/cgi-bin/New/facs/5930

155. GODLEE F, GALE CR, MARTYN CN. Effect on the quality of peer review of blinding reviewers and asking them to sign their reports: A randomized controlled trial. *Journal of the American Medical Association* 1998; 280:237–40.

156. LAWRENCE ALTMAN, personal communication, Sept 30, 1999.

157. LEVI R. Overshooting the target. *Science and Practice* 1995, no. 2.

158. The Cardiac Arrhythmia Pilot Study (CAPS) Investigators. Effects of encainide, flecainide, imipramine, and moricizine on ventricular arrhythmias during the year after acute myocardial infarction: The CAPS. *American Journal of Cardiology* 1988; 61:501–9.

159. FLEMING TR, DEMETS DL. Surrogate end points in clinical trials: Are we being misled? *Annals of Internal Medicine* 1996; 125:605–13.

160. ECHT DS ET AL. Mortality and morbidity in patients receiving encainide, flecainide, or placebo: The Cardiac Arrhythmia Suppression Trial. *New England Journal of Medicine* 1991; 324:781–88.

161. GØTZSCHE PC, LIBERATI A, TORRI V, ROSSETTI L. Beware of surrogate outcome measures. *International Journal of Technology Assessment in Health Care* 1996; 12:238–46.

162. *Undertaking systematic reviews of research on effectiveness: CRD guidelines for those carrying out or commissioning reviews.* CRD Report no. 4. York: University of York, NHS Centre for Reviews and Dissemination, 1996.

163. GREENHALGH, T. How to read a paper: Papers that report drug trials. *British Medical Journal* 1997; 315:480–83.

164. LEVI R. För patienten är helheten viktigast [Interview]. *Vetenskap & praxis* 1995, no. 1.

165. DR. PAUL HJEMDAHL, associate professor and clinical pharmacologist at the Karolinska Institute, Sweden, personal communication, Feb 1998.

166. ALTMAN LK. Bringing news to the public: The role of the media. In Warren KS, Mosteller F (eds). Doing more good than harm: The evaluation of health care interventions. *Annals of the New York Academy of Sciences* 1993; 703:204.

167. Moderately elevated blood pressure: A report from SBU, the Swedish Council on Technology Assessment in Health Care. *Journal of Internal Medicine* 1995; 238 suppl 737:1–225.

168. *Måttligt förhöjt blodtryck.* SBU Report no. 121, Stockholm: SBU, 1994, updated 1998.

169. LEVI R. Really, is anyone healthy? [Interview]. *Science and Practice* 1995, no. 2.

170. PRESCOTT-CLARKE P, MOSTYN BJ. Public attitudes towards the acceptability of risks. In Prescott-Clarke P (ed). *Public attitudes towards industrial, work-related and other risks.* London: Social and Community Planning Research, 1982.

171. CALMAN KC, ROYSTON G. Risk language and dialects. *British Medical Journal* 1997; 315:939–42.

172. PALING J. *Up to your armpits in alligators: How to sort out what risks are worth worrying about!* Florida: Risk Communication and Environmental Institute, 1993.

173. PAULOS JA. *Innumeracy.* Harmondsworth: Penguin, 1990.

174. ALTMAN LK. The Ingelfinger rule, embargoes, and journal peer review. Part 1. *Lancet* 1996; 347:1382–86.

175. HARTZ J, CHAPPELL R. *Worlds apart.* Nashville: Freedom Forum First Amendment Center, Vanderbuilt University, 1997.

176. SCHWITZER G. The magical medical media tour [Commentary]. *Journal of the American Medical Association* 1992; 267:1969–71.

177. HANSEN KA, WARD J, CONNERS JL, NEUZIL M. Local breaking news: Sources, technology, and news routines. *Journalism Quarterly* 1994; 71:566–69.

178. FINER D, TOMSON G. Medicines in the news: Content analysis of drug articles in four Vietnamese newspapers. *International Journal of Risk and Safety in Medicine* 1999; accepted for publication.

179. STRYER DB, LURIE P, BERO LA. Dear doctor . . . regarding calcium channel blockers [Letter]. *Journal of the American Medical Association* 1996; 275:517–19.

180. HORTON R. Spinning the risks and benefits of calcium antagonists. *Lancet* 1995; 346: 586–87.

181. PISETSKY DS. The breakthrough. *Annals of Internal Medicine* 1996; 124:345–47.

182. WINSTEN JA. Science and the media: The boundaries of truth. *Health Affairs* 1985; 4:5–23.

183. *NASW Newsletter*, Mar 1966.

184. CREWDSON J. Perky cheerleaders. *Nieman Reports* 1993; 47:11–16.

185. KLAIDMAN S, BEAUCHAMP TL. The virtuous journalist: Morality in journalism. In Cohen ED (ed). *Philosophical issues in journalism.* New York: Oxford University Press, 1992.

186. SERENA STOCKWELL, personal communication, Sept 28, 1999.

187. Website maintained by the Center for the Study of Ethics in the Profession (CSEP) at the Illinois Institute of Technology, http://csep.iit.edu/codes/media.html, accessed on Feb 28, 2000.

188. Website of the U.S. Federal Trade Commission, http://www.ftc.gov/bcp/conline/pubs/alerts/mrclalrt.htm, accessed on Dec 5, 1999.

189. ALTMAN LK. Promises of miracles: News releases go where journals fear to tread; a double standard in reports to the public and the experts. *New York Times*, Jan 10, 1995.

190. BERO LA, JADAD AR. How consumers and policymakers can use systematic reviews for decision making. *Annals of Internal Medicine* 1997; 127:37–42.

191. BASTIAN H. Finding out what health care works: Consumer involvement in research and the Cochrane Collaboration [Editorial]. *Health Forum* 1994; 32:15–16.

192. HUNT DL, MCKIBBON KA. Locating and appraising systematic reviews. *Annals of Internal Medicine* 1997; 126:532–38.

193. PHILLIPS K, BERO LA. Improving the use of information in medical effectiveness research. *International Journal of Quality in Health Care* 1996; 8:21–30.

194. BARNES D, BERO L. Quality of review articles on environmental tobacco smoke [Abstract]. New York: American Public Health Association Meeting, 1996.

195. SPURGEON D. Canadian GPs believe that media health reporting could be better [News]. *British Medical Journal* 1999; 318:1578.

196. STOCKING SH, GROSS PH. How do journalists think? A proposal for the study of cognitive bias in newsmaking. Bloomington, IN: ERIC Clearinghouse on Reading and Communication Skills, 1989.

197. STOCKING SH, GROSS PH. Understanding errors and biases that can affect journalists. In Cohen ED (ed). *Philosophical issues in journalism.* New York: Oxford University Press, 1992.

198. BLAND JM, ALTMAN DG. Some examples of regression towards the mean. *British Medical Journal* 1994; 309:780.

199. JONES EE, HARRIS VA. The attribution of attitudes. *Journal of Experimental Social Psychology* 1967; 3:1–24.

200. BROAD W, WADE N. *Betrayers of the truth: Fraud and deceit in the halls of science.* New York, NY: Simon and Schuster, 1982.

201. HAIMAN B. 10 Plagues on the 4th estate . . . and how to stop them. Published on Poynter Institute Website, http://www.poynter.org/research/compcred/cred_BHspeech.htm, accessed on Nov 2, 1999.

202. GRIFFIN RJ. Using systematic thinking to choose and evaluate evidence. In Friedman SM, Dunwoody S, Rogers CL (eds). *Communicating uncertainty: Media coverage of new and controversial science.* Mahwah, NJ: Lawrence Erlbaum Associates, 1999.

203. COHN V. Reporters as gatekeepers. In Moore M (ed). *Health risks and the press: Perspectives on media coverage of risk assessment and health.* Washington, DC: Media Institute and the American Medical Association, 1989.

204. KLAIDMAN S. *Health in the headlines: The stories behind the stories.* New York, NY: Oxford University Press, 1991

205. PINI P. Media wars. *Lancet* 1995; 346:1681–83.

206. ANGELL M. *Science on trial: The clash between medical science and the law in the breast implant case.* New York, NY: Norton, 1996.

207. GILBERT. D. *Direct-to-consumer advertising of prescription medicines.* SCRIP report. Richmond, Surrey: PJB Publications, 1998.

208. ANONYMOUS. Hooking the punter. *Economist,* Aug 26, 1995.

209. IMS HEALTH, INC., 1999, http://imshealth.com/html/news_arc/04_21_1999_195.htm, accessed on Oct 22, 1999.

210. PhRMA Website, http://www.phrma.org/facts/bkgrndr/advert.html, document dated Sept 21, 1999, and accessed on Nov 3, 1999.

211. Public Citizen's Health Research Group Website, http://www.citizen.org/hrg/PUBLICA-TIONS/1400.htm, document dated Aug 12, 1996, and accessed on Nov 3, 1999.

212. CARNALL, D. Website of the week: Drug advertising. *British Medical Journal* 1999; 319:1208.

213. MARCHANT D. *Pharmaceutical marketing strategies on the Internet.* SCRIP report. Richmond, Surrey: PJB Publications, 1997.

214. Council Directive 92/28/EEC, of 31 Mar 1992, on the advertising of medicinal products for human use. Accessible on European Commission Website, http://dg3.eudra.org/eudralex/vol-1/home.htm

215. MILLER MW. Creating a buzz: With remedy in hand, drug firms get ready to popularize illness. *Wall Street Journal,* Apr 27, 1994.

216. FISHER P, WARD A, Complementary medicine in Europe. *British Medical Journal* 1994; 309:107–11.

217. EISENBERG DM, KESSLER RC, FOSTER C, ET AL. Unconventional medicine in the United States: Prevalence, costs, and patterns of use. *New England Journal of Medicine* 1993; 328:246–52.

218. ANGELL M, KASSIRER JP. Alternative medicine: The risks of untested and unregulated remedies [Editorial]. *New England Journal of Medicine* 1998; 339:830–41.

219. SLIFMAN NR, OBERMEYER WR, ALOI BK, ET AL. Contamination of botanical dietary supplements by *Digitalis lanata. New England Journal of Medicine* 1998; 339:806–11.

220. KO RJ. Adulterants in Asian patent medicines. *New England Journal of Medicine* 1998; 339:847.

221. LOVECCHIO F, CURRY SC, BAGNASCO T. Butyrolactone-induced central nervous system depression after ingestion of RenewTrient, a "dietary supplement." *New England Journal of Medicine* 1998; 339:847–48.

222. BEIGEL Y, OSTFELD I, SCHOENFELD N. A leading question. *New England Journal of Medicine* 1998; 339:827–30.

223. STEHLIN IB. An FDA guide to choosing medical treatments. FDA Consumer, June 1995. Published on FDA Website, http://www.fda.gov/oashi/aids/fdaguide.html, accessed on Oct 25, 1999.

224. Herbal roulette. *Consumer Reports*, Nov 1995, p. 698.
225. CUI J, GARLE M, ENEROTH P, BJORKHEM I. What do commercial ginseng preparations contain? *Lancet* 1994; 344:134.
226. NICHOLAS WADE, personal communication, Oct 14, 1999.
227. GRAYSON L. *Scientific deception: An overview and guide to the literature of misconduct and fraud in scientific research*. London: British Library, 1995.
228. SAVAN B. *Science under siege: The myth of objectivity in scientific research*. Montreal: CBC Enterprises, 1988.
229. EYSENBACH G, SA ER, DIEPGEN TL. Shopping around the Internet today and tomorrow: Towards the millennium of cybermedicine. *British Medical Journal* 1999; 319:1294.
230. Health on the Net Foundation. HON's fourth survey on the use of the Internet for medical and health purposes, published on Website, http://www.hon.ch/Survey/Resume Apr99.html, accessed on Dec 5, 1999.
231. Graphics, Visualization and Usability (GVU) Center at Georgia Tech College of Computing. GVU's 10th WWW User Survey, published on Website, http://www.cc.gatech.edu/gvu/user_surveys/survey-1998-10/, accessed on Dec 5, 1999.
232. LEVI R. Risk för desinformation på Internet: Kvalitetsmärkning av medicinska hemsidor prövas [Risk of disinformation on the Internet: Quality labeling of medical Websites is tested]. *Läkartidningen* 1999; 96:1737–40.
233. KILEY R. *Medical information on the Internet: A guide for health professionals*. Second edition. Glasgow: Churchill Livingstone, 1999.
234. EYSENBACH G, DIEPGEN TL. Towards quality management of medical information on the Internet: Evaluating, labelling, and filtering of information. *British Medical Journal* 1998; 317:1496–1500.
235. SHEPPERD S, CHARNOCK D, GANN B. Helping patients access high quality health information. *British Medical Journal* 1999; 319:764–66.
236. GUSTAFSON DH, ROBINSON TN, ANSLEY D, ADLER L, BRENNAN PF, for the Science Panel on Interactive Communication and Health. Consumers and evaluation of interactive health communication applications. *American Journal of Preventive Medicine* 1999; 16:23–29.
237. URETSKY, S. Beware of useless or dangerous medical advice on-line. *Internet World*, Feb 1996.
238. BOWER, H. Internet sees growth of unverified health claims. *British Medical Journal* 1996; 313:381.
239. LARKIN, M. Internet accelerates spread of bogus cancer cure [Media Review]. *Lancet* 1999; 353:331.
240. Federal Trade Commission of the United States. Consumer alert: Virtual "treatments" can be real world deceptions. Published on June 1999 on FTC Website, http://www.ftc.gov/bcp/conline/pubs/alerts/mrclalrt.htm, accessed on Dec 5, 1999.
241. BRODY J. Point-and-click medicine: A hazard to your health. *New York Times*, Aug 31, 1999.
242. ANONYMOUS. Internet alert: FTC warns against false health claims. CNN, June 24, 1999.
243. ANONYMOUS. Internet can be quick link to bad health information. CNN, July 29, 1999.
244. IMPICCIATORE P, PANDOLFINI C, CASELLA N, BONATI M. Reliability of health information for the public on the World Wide Web: Systematic survey of advice on managing fever in children at home. *British Medical Journal* 1997; 314:1875–79.
245. BIERMANN JS, GOLLADAY GJ, GREENFIELD ML, BAKER LH. Evaluation of cancer information on the Internet. *Cancer* 1999; 86:381–90.
246. DE BOUSINGEN DD. Austrian cancer patient's parents sentenced [News]. *Lancet* 1996; 348:1440.

247. NIGEL G. German "quack healer" arrested [News]. *Lancet* 1997; 349:1679.
248. DE BOUSINGEN DD. German "quack healer" sentenced [News]. *Lancet* 1997; 350:874.
249. SILBERG WM, LUNDBERG GD, MUSACCHIO RA. Assessing, controlling, and assuring the quality of medical information on the Internet. *Journal of the American Medical Association* 1997; 277:1244–45.
250. KIM P, ENG TR, DEERING MJ, MAXFIELD A. Published criteria for evaluating health related Websites: Review. *British Medical Journal* 1999; 318:647–49.
251. National Institutes of Health Website, http://www.nih.gov/welcome/director/pubmedcentral/pubmedcentral.htm, published on Aug 30, 1999, accessed on Nov 16, 1999.
252. CARUSO D. The law and the Internet. *Columbia Journalism Review* 1998; 37:57–60.
253. SCHULTE HH, DUFRESNE MP. *Getting the story: An advanced reporting guide to beats, records, and sources.* Needham Heights, MA: Macmillan Publishing Co, 1994.
254. BLACK J. Areopagitica in the information age. *Journal of Mass Media Ethics* 1994; 9:131–34.
255. *United Nations Development Program. Human development report 1998.* New York: Oxford University Press, 1999.
256. NUA Ltd. NUA Internet Surveys, Sept 1999, published on Website, http://www.nua.ie/surveys/how_many_online/index.html, accessed on Dec 5, 1999.
257. QUICK, R. Web journalists are finding themselves out of the loop. *Wall Street Journal,* Aug 14, 1997, p. B9.
258. WHITE DM. The "gate keeper": A case study in the selection of news. *Journalism Quarterly* 1950; 27:383–90.
259. JANOWITZ M. Professional models in journalism: The gatekeeper and the advocate. *Journalism Quarterly* 1975; 52:618–26, 662.
260. SINGER JB. Online journalists: Foundations for research into their changing roles. *Journal of Computer-Mediated Communication,* Sept 1998. Published on Website http://www.ascusc.org/jcmc/vol4/issue1/singer.html, accessed on Dec 8, 1999.
261. MOYNIHAN R, BERO L, ROSS-DEGNAN D, HENRY D, LEE K, WATKINS J, MAH C, SOUMERAI SB. Coverage by the news media of the benefits and risks of medications. *New England Journal of Medicine* 2000; 342:1645–50.
262. ENTWISTLE VA, WATT IS. Judging journalism: How should the quality of news reporting about clinical interventions be assessed and improved? *Quality in Health Care* 1999; 8:172–76.
263. Cybercitizen Health 2000, survey by Cyber Dialogue, quoted on the company's Website, http://www.cyberdialogue.com/news/releases/2000/08-22-cch-launch.html, published on Aug 22, 2000, accessed on Jan 13, 2001.
264. FRIEDMAN TL. Foreign affairs: At God's elbow. *New York Times,* Apr 10, 1996.

Index